T0194062

Endorsements

Author and sister-in-law Beth Banning skillfully painted moving honest portraits of the men God brought into her life; however, not with the stroke of a brush using oil or acrylics, but rather perfectly illustrated the pages of this book with her gift of words. For anyone in pursuit of finding their Prince Charming, I highly recommend "*When the Glass Slipper Breaks*" as inspiration in discovering their ultimate soul mate.

David A. Green, President/CEO
PBH RESIDENTIAL CARE HOMES

Thank you, Jesus, for bringing Cinderella into my life. As usual, your timing was perfect. After a major promotion and the daunting task of overhauling a marketing and sales department, you provided the Diamond needed to guarantee success. She was anything but ordinary. There was no doubt Big Daddy and her Dad would be so proud. Her work ethic was amazing. Her positive can-do attitude was incredible. Her writing skills are the best I have ever seen. Most of all her integrity and trust in the Lord were present every day. Thank you, Cinderella, for being part of my family.

God Bless, Terry Thach
Business Owner

Beth Banning's compact and insightful book is ideal for anyone to read especially women. Beth does a great job keeping the reader's attention as she prompts her audience to consider the impact men have had in their life. I had chills when I read how God used me as an instrument in her life. I've got to believe anyone reading Beth's story, whether mature or young in the faith will find much to meditate and reflect on in their own life's journey. Her story is a great reminder to all of us that we can achieve "the sparkling diamonds of love, joy, peace, longsuffering, gentleness, goodness, faith, temperance and meekness." Beth challenges us to focus on the eternal perspective and not allow our temporal circumstances to define who we are.

All for His Glory, Jeff Haddock
Business Owner

When the Glass Slipper Breaks

OVERCOMING
BROKEN
RELATIONSHIPS

Beth Banning

WESTBOW
PRESS®
A DIVISION OF THOMAS NELSON
& ZONDERVAN

WestBow Press books may be ordered through booksellers or by contacting:

WestBow Press
A Division of Thomas Nelson & Zondervan
1663 Liberty Drive
Bloomington, IN 47403
www.westbowpress.com
1 (866) 928-1240

ISBN: 978-1-9736-1958-1 (sc)
ISBN: 978-1-9736-1959-8 (hc)
ISBN: 978-1-9736-1957-4 (e)

Library of Congress Control Number: 2018901839

Print information available on the last page.

WestBow Press rev. date: 02/14/2018

Contents

Foreword

What an amazing forte author Beth Banning summoned in chronicling attributes learned through a lifetime from the men God placed in her life in *"When the Glass Slipper Breaks."* With precise skill, she discerned character qualities from a point of view of pure innocence and genuine naivete to discover the secrets of male/female relationships. Learn, she did. Then as a young woman thrust into the complexities of life with societal turmoil, finding maturity and strength of heart and mind to commence a search for her Prince Charming is remarkable.

Her exposes are authentic, interesting, and purposeful leading the reader to want to be her shadow companion on this worthy pursuit. And just when one thinks the glass slipper is forever broken and all is hopeless…the glorious discovery is revealed! This beautiful and honest narrative will guide a searching heart through various destinations of *Fairytale Dreams, Hard Realities, Broken Hearts, Practical Certainties,* and *Heavenly Bliss.*

Terri Green
Owner & COO
PBH Residential Care Homes

Preface

In her book *The Cinderella Syndrome*, Lee Ezell talks about America's propensity (particularly the baby boomer generation) to live in a fairy tale. Raised on Walt Disney fantasies in a post-war era, my generation was given the world on a silver platter. Good had just prevailed over evil in World War II, the economy was better than it had ever been, and women were finding themselves in a whole new light of self-worth and value. Modern technology was producing marvels such as color TV, the electric range, and small appliances. Extraordinary talk about man going to the moon brought light to our eyes as we believed anything was possible.

Just as our generation dared to begin dreaming the American dream, the onslaught of the '60s torpedoed our hopes with the Vietnam war, the assassinations of President Kennedy, Robert Kennedy and Martin Luther King; and the rebellion of a generation that was so indulged it couldn't deal with life on any level. Our hearts began to beat to the rhythm of a different drummer with modern ideals and illusions of grandeur primarily found in drugs. Deep down inside, however, women everywhere still harbored the gnawing dream of a Prince Charming with the romantic notion that the perfect one with the lost slipper would find us and rescue our hearts.

For the women of my generation, the final outcome was not pretty. Many resorted to the women's liberation movement and forfeited their dreams to a political ideal that in many ways sold their souls to bitterness. Many drowned in cynicism and despair, losing their capacity to love and be loved. Many succumbed to their parents' way of life, always looking for the niche their parents had and never knowing the real extent of their relationships. Many experienced abuses from a generation of men who had lost their identity through the circumstances of life. All the while, women wondered what happened to the Cinderella dream. Less than half could find solace in the arms of a man they would commit to for life.

Dismal as it may sound, my generation of women came home with a broken slipper and gave their best to survive the heartbreak. With America's divorce rate climbing, at least four generations have come and gone without the capacity to dream for a Prince Charming to find them … without the capacity to discover the innocence of their youth. After all, why bother to dream when it will never come true? Why even build yourself up only to be let down? Why pretend to believe it could ever happen to you?

For you, dear reader, the permission to dream again is there for the taking. There is a way to muddle through the heartache of a broken heart and come out on top. Life truly is wonderful, and love is worth fighting for. There is a promise of hope that can make you the George Bailey of your circumstances. To get there, we just need to know what to do *When the Glass Slipper Breaks.*

It is my prayer that by the end of this book, you can dare to dream once again.

Beth Banning

CHAPTER 1

Once Upon a Time

"Once upon a time, there lived an ordinary girl."

In their screenplay *Ever After*, Andy Tennant, Susannah Grant, and Rick Parks take us back to the origins of the Cinderella story. Drew Barrymore plays a young, ordinary girl who is raised by her widowed father and is the apple of his eye. All of his affections are bestowed on her and her alone until he falls in love with the wicked stepmother. Her dad then suddenly dies, leaving her to be raised by a woman who hates her.

Ordinary girls everywhere went to see this classic film with a twist, which grossed over $65 million domestically and $35 million in foreign theaters. For some reason, the American public was captivated by the hope that dreams really can come true in spite of the havoc American culture has wreaked on the institution of marriage and on strong relationships.

This ordinary girl in the modern-day Cinderella story unassumingly found her favorite book to be *Utopia*—not necessarily because of its meaning as much as because it was the last book her father had given her. Her plans of growing up to become a wife and mother—in that order, of course—were cemented in the love her father had for her.

As we build on our relationships, very few women consider the influence their fathers have on their choice of men. According to the Fatherhood Initiative, statistics tell us that over twenty-four million children live without their biological fathers in their homes. As fathers become increasingly absent from children's lives, girls are more insecure and more likely to have skewed ideas of marriage and love. They begin seeking acceptance through sexual promiscuity and abhorrent behavior to attract anyone to love them.

In my case, it was difficult to find anyone who measured up to my father. Because I lost him to a premature death when I was only eighteen years of age, I had virtually no one to compare him to when seeking my soul mate. However, I had a rich heritage of men in my family, which gave me a foundation for what to look for in a man.

We have probably all seen a picture of Norman Rockwell's grandfather with the little girl sitting on his lap or teaching the little boy the joys of fishing. Carry that picture, if possible, to the real grandfather figures in our lives who gave us the foundation for what to seek in a soul mate. My grandfathers were the epitome of virtue and holy faith. They were great men of previous generations who lived for right and died with the freedom to do what was right. They lived in simpler times that made white-framed houses into castles and picket fences into fortresses. They were patriots of a greater America who stood for God, country, and the American way, and they were firsthand witnesses to the horrors of a world at war. They participated in the victory over the greatest threats ever known to our country—communism and Nazi Germany.

Do you have someone in your life who was a grandfather to you, either literally or figuratively? Did you know your grandfather? Were you close to him? How has he influenced your choice of men? It was my destiny to personally know my grandfathers only through the lives of those they touched. My dad's father died of a heart attack just a few months after I was born. My mom's dad was struck by a drunk driver several years prior and was instantly killed. I am acquainted with them from the pictures that line my hallway, mirroring the image of the men they were and the characteristics they inculcated into my parents.

My paternal grandfather was a tall, strong man who always wore a smile. He married a small, frail woman who adored him long after his death. His work ethic was impeccable as he poured blood, sweat, and tears into the railroad lines and brought in a new era of transportation for the state of Texas. From the humid forests of Huntsville to the stretching pines of Palestine, he laid the rails of the twentieth century.

My dad learned his solid work ethic at the feet of his dad, and I learned its value through him. I learned early on that laziness in a man promises poverty and an empty life. That was instilled in me as I watched my dad replicate what he had learned from his father. If it was broken, he fixed it. Whether it was his job or not, he did what he could to get the job done. If he saw something that needed to be done, he did it. There was no ranking or pecking order in my grandfather's work ethic. He embraced the idea of helping others and getting the job done, pursuing excellence along the way.

My grandfather was a man's man, cut from the cloth of human decency and wrapped in the cloak of brotherly kindness. He carried his craft to heights of excellence and rose through the ranks of his profession with integrity and example. His exemplary person was not only seen in the eyes of his peers but also felt in the heart of his family. He was a strong disciplinarian with a gentle touch. His word could stop the foulest argument, and his touch could soothe the most troubled soul. That's how my dad learned to discipline us. My grandfather loved his parents and family, as evidenced in the continuous sacrifice he made to care for his mother and twelve siblings until the day he died.

My grandfather found joy in putting his Lord first, others second, and himself last. He was a man of prayer and everyone knew where he was at 10:00 pm. His prayer closet was in the upstairs apartment window seat. There, he interceded for all he knew; and it was felt by friends and family alike. It produced a gentleness in him that knew when to stand up and fight and when to be sensitive to the needs of a woman. Through his example, it became important for me early on to understand that being a gentleman was one of those timeless attributes that cannot be dismissed. We can learn a lot from the greatest generation when looking for men to share in our lives. If we forego looking for a gentleman, we invite abuse and heartache.

With each announcement of new grandchildren, my grandfather began immediately carrying on the tradition of making that special keepsake passed down from grandfather to grandchild. His incredible skill in ironworks produced a small iron stove and a wrought iron baby bed for my sisters. For my brother, he made an authentic pitchfork and shovel. And for me, he made an iron cross with a stair-step pedestal, which is a cherished memento of his legacy to this day.

Probably one of the most important lessons I learned in looking for men to share in my life was to look at their personal legacies. Who were their parents? How did they treat their moms? What were their attitudes toward those who had passed down their heritage? My grandfather loved the idea of living long after he was gone. He ensured we shared a piece of him physically, spiritually, emotionally, and intellectually. He lives on even today in the lives of my grandchildren because he was considerate of leaving a lasting legacy that he cared about.

PaPa respected life and brought meaning to the honor of fatherhood. He passed down his name without reproach as a shining torch to the next generation. From his life's witness, I learned the power of a good name. And when looking for a man of my dreams, I remembered from his testimony that a good name is better than silver or gold.

How do we know a man has a good name? Finding out the reputation he has at work, in social circles, within his family, and among his acquaintances helps introduce us to his nobility (or lack thereof). How does he handle his money, and what does he do with his resources? These are all characteristics that indicate the name he will pass down to his children. They exemplify how he will live on long after he is gone, and it was my grandfather's life legacy that made my dad the great man he was.

My maternal grandfather was born into poverty and died at the hands of moral bankruptcy when the drunken son of the city mayor struck him down and abandoned the scene of the crime. My grandfather represented the meek of the earth and was a quiet, timid man who survived insurmountable odds. Unable to complete school due to financial hardship, he returned to receive his high school diploma at the age of twenty-one. His mind was brilliant, and he always aspired to become an attorney. His favorite pastime was political discussion.

Too many times, women think the most important aspect of our relationships is chemistry or attraction. We tend to dismiss any man who doesn't have the "spark" we are looking for. Those are the visible areas in building a relationship that are important; however, if the inner man is impoverished, the outer man will soon fade into oblivion. I have thought many times about the boy who struck and killed my grandfather. What do you think became of him? He was never held accountable for his crime. Did he learn from that experience? Did it haunt him the rest of his life? Did it sear his conscience so much that day that he couldn't get it back? What kind of man did he become? How did that one moment in time affect his relationships?

Affectionately known as Big Daddy by his grandchildren, my grandfather struggled all of his life to make ends meet. His industrious spirit created within him a versatile career path that would cover the scope of virtually every trade in the South. He was a cotton gin owner, a rancher, and an oil supervisor, traveling everywhere from the wild plains of Texas to the white sands of New Mexico to get work. His work ethic was unquenchable, and he became a model of perseverance to those who watched his life.

In seeking out the men I wanted in my life, perseverance became increasingly important to me. How was he faithful? Did he love something so much that he would persevere to achieve success? Where did his passions lie? I hoped that the spiritual was central to his life, because it was so important to me. If he couldn't be faithful to God, how could he be faithful to me?

Like my grandfather, his wife was dedicated and faithful not only to him but to her Lord and His church. Having four children, my grandfather spent the rest of his life supporting his family any way he could. Being an independent businessman, he owned several cotton gins, two of which burned down. On one of those occasions, having a compassionate heart for the transients of his day, he allowed many homeless people to take shelter in his gins at night. One morning he awoke only to find that his gin had burned to the ground, completely gutting the building and everything in it. He lost everything. Insurance was not even a consideration in those days, and restoring what was lost became the responsibility of the owner.

Looking to find a new beginning anywhere he could, he moved ahead of his family to New Mexico, leaving them with loved ones until he could send for them. He rebuilt another gin from the ground up in 1928, but a stronger competitor and the pending stock market crash took him to bankruptcy the following winter.

There are so many positive attributes to look for in a man, but it is equally as important to look for the circumstances that bring a man down. How does he deal with the issues of life that are unfair, unjust, and immoral? What defeats him or causes him to fall into depression? How much stock does he put into his job, his family, his friends? Are these areas of life that my strengths can complement to bring about a fullness of life?

In all of the times they spent apart, it was never in the mind of my grandfather to be unfaithful to his wife or to abandon his responsibility to his children. Many women forfeit the pleasure of fidelity in a man for a personality that is not conducive to faithfulness. That was not the case with my grandfather. In spite of overwhelming circumstances, his commitment was strong and his vision was bright. He believed in the perseverance of the human spirit and stayed young at heart until his death. It was the depths of his love that took my grandmother through thirty-five years of widowhood, never to remarry.

His memory taught me to look to the inner man of faith and dedication; when looking for a man to marry, I searched high and low for a man who was more committed to the Lord Jesus Christ than to me. I wanted a man who, like my grandfather, would be faithful to me during the most adverse circumstances of life and whose love would burn for me no matter what.

It was my good fortune to have a foundation upon which to build my image of what to look for in a man. Even though I was young, I remember thinking about what I wanted in my Prince Charming, and of course, he had to be like those men God had already used to pioneer the love bug within me. Naturally, turning to my father as a living example stayed emblazoned in my heart as I watched firsthand what a man should be.

Pierre Curie once said, "All great men are pure and simple." Such was true of my father. Without knowing it sometimes, the primary man in every girl's life is her daddy. Regardless of how our dads have failed us, fundamental to every girl's being is her father. I've lived many years as a single parent, and without exception, my daughter's dad was excused of whatever "sin" he imposed upon her. In spite of full knowledge regarding his shortcomings and the many reasons why, she invariably forgave him of anything.

These seem to be innate feelings a girl has for her father whether she knows him or not. That truth is seen in many adopted children who end up seeking their birth fathers, whether the results are good or bad. Looking at my dad through the eyes of memories long since faded, one thing crystal clear to my thinking was his infallibility. He was a gentle, kind man with an insatiable love for family. It was very difficult for Dad to communicate because of his immense shyness, but a smile never left his face, and his laugh never failed to amuse us all. In fact, it has been said of my father that he died laughing. He had reared his head back in laughter to a joke my uncle had told when his heart failed and he slumped down, falling to the floor. He would never again regain consciousness.

When women are asked about the top three characteristics they look for in a man, a sense of humor always makes the list. My dad loved to laugh. Laughter is medicine to the soul and can heal many wounds of the heart. Unfortunately, women have mistaken this attribute for a stand-up comedian or someone with a quick wit. It is easy to forget that joy comes from the soul and is a fruit of the Holy Spirit. A man who walks with God can generate this characteristic without having the personality to perform. A joyful man brings light to any situation and can blanket our lives with peace. In the same token, a negative, critical man can break our spirits and destroy our homes.

My dad raised five teenagers in the midst of the turbulent '60s and '70s and watched his children experience some remarkable victories and defeats. He never failed to advise us to "give him his walking papers" if our boyfriends weren't measuring up to his standard. It was his silent strength that empowered us with self-confidence and a sense of security until he left us entirely too soon.

He took on the arduous task of leading a scout troop for several years and taught America's young men allegiance to honor and integrity. It was important to him to instill in a generation of men the importance of keeping their word.

He was a faithful deacon at our church and superintended a department of middle school kids for several years until his health prevented it. Despite his inability to communicate well, he consistently stood every Sunday morning in front of a group of adolescent boys expounding the truth of God's Word and life's purpose for men. He became a shining star of manhood for many boys whose fathers had failed them. Even today, when those he taught are asked of the impact he made on their lives, only glowing reports follow.

He worked for almost thirty years at a technological firm and faced the rigorous challenge of an ever-changing technology. His brilliant mind met that challenge, and as a result, he maintained supervisory positions throughout his career there. He was a superlative employee and loyal to an employer that I believe never knew what they had. He always considered himself ordinary in terms of this world's power and prestige, but his greatness bore out in a life well lived.

It was during those days when his kids were young and there were seven hungry mouths to feed that my dad had to decide whether to work on Sunday. Begrudgingly, he made the decision to acquiesce to his employer's whims. After only a few months, he took a demotion to ensure he could be present on the Lord's Day. It was one of those "forever" memories for me as I realized the importance of being a spiritual testimony to my kids.

I know spirituality has been pushed down the list of priorities when looking to share life with a man. As a women's ministry leader for over twenty years, however, I have witnessed considerable devastation that women have suffered because they overlooked this important trait. Why is it that we feed the spirit least? We are created in the image of God with minds, bodies, and souls. We take great measures to maintain strong physical bodies. We spend thousands to educate our minds and find unique and interesting ways to sharpen them. But our spirits can be starved and depleted until they cry out in the center of our beings for attention. The man who nourishes his spirit as a priority is a man who will be stronger in all other aspects of life.

It never occurred to me to question our father or his intentions because they were obvious. He always stood for right and carried out the principles of high morals and integrity. Without exception, when my dad spoke, we listened! Even though he was meek and mild-mannered, his voice could thunder out, shaking the walls to a deafening silence. He brought stability to an unstable time in our lives and labored relentlessly to meet the needs and desires of five children who could never appreciate all he gave.

My father was, to me, the epitome of a gentleman. His manners were above reproach, and his adulation for womanhood never ceased. Having seen the ravages of Hitler's genocide on the Jewish people and the horrendous results of Japanese torture in WWII, he still maintained a gentleness that never let those memories invade his person. Instead, he expressed himself in genteel ways and with an artistic mind.

When my dad wanted to be alone and out of the clutter and confusion of a huge family, he channeled his frustrations and anxieties by closing himself up in the garage and creating something positive. Women tend to ignore the need for men to have an outlet. We are so focused on our lives' fulfillment that we forget the need for men to spend some time in the garage alone, go out with male friends for fellowship, enjoy a men's Bible study, or simply let their creative juices flow through chosen hobbies.

During his alone time, my dad created some of the most beautiful pieces of woodwork anyone could imagine. He could turn a normal piece of wood into a masterpiece in the form of furniture, a Bible holder, or anything that was in the mind of my mother to make for Christmas that year. His creative flair lined the hallways of our junior high room at church, and our church enjoyed many podiums at the hands of a master designer. I never heard my father speak a curse word or saw him drink a drop of liquor. Those demons would never enter the haven of our home if he had anything to say about it.

Since I witnessed firsthand the consistent goodness of a man so loved during the beginning years of my life, it was impossible to forget the possibility that there was good in men. In projecting that image, my father gave me the image of our heavenly Father, who promises to meet our needs and hear our cries and is the same yesterday, today, and forever. Goodness was my earthly father's identity, and his steps were truly ordered of the Lord. It was his example that kept me looking for a faithful man of integrity.

When he passed away, the essence of his life was spelled out in the flyleaf of his Bible:

> *My Consecration*
> *I am willing:*
> *To receive what Thou giveth,*
> *To lack what Thou withholdeth,*
> *To relinquish what Thou taketh,*
> *To suffer what Thou inflicteth,*
> *To be what Thou requireth,*
> *To do what Thou commandeth.*

What pictures do you have of your heavenly Father because of your relationship with your earthly father? The answer to that question is the key to a successful relationship since every union in life depends upon our relationship with our heavenly Father.

I would be remiss not to mention the impact these seemingly "perfect" men had on the lives of their sons. Both my uncle and my brother struggled to meet such a standard and made choices that would haunt them for the rest of their lives. Perhaps expecting perfection from men is too much to ask when seeking a life mate, but women who can be a help meet to a man in areas of weakness can sharpen the strength of men no matter their failings.

Born into a middle class American Christian family, I was raised in '50s suburbia, which by today's standards is considered Cinderella's utopia. My parents loved one another and were married for thirty years until death took my dad. Contrary to what kids experience today, we shared our rooms with siblings and shared one bathroom with the whole family. We went to Sunday school and church every Sunday and enjoyed Bible studies on Wednesday evenings. We *never* asked if we could stay home from church. That was carved into our schedules like stone.

Going out to eat was a luxury for a family of seven, and purchasing a new dress from the store was an exception. My mother sewed everything we wore, and I couldn't wait to get my sisters' hand-me-downs. We lived in too close quarters not to learn from one another, and our parents made very clear the consequences of our choices, whether right or wrong.

How was that utopia? Living in a world of black and white gave me a point of reference when everything became gray in the '60s. The Word of God was and is the standard of truth, and no one in our circle would ever veer from what the Bible said. There was a definite hedge of protection around our family during those turbulent years for that very reason. While other families were clinging to temporal values and things that did not last, my parents and our church family made sure we held fast to the Rock of our Salvation, Jesus Christ.

Every one of us have a story to tell of our fathers and the men who molded and shaped our idea of relationships with men. My life sounds perfect compared to girls whose grandfathers and fathers have molested or abandoned them. According to Child Help, over six million children are reported physically and/or sexually abused every year in the United States.[1] Those repercussions produce mental disorders that are rarely treated. Either girls grow up and look for relationships that pattern after their relationship with their father or the opposite of that with their father. Either way, if they have not worked through their own abuse, it can cause devastating effects in any relationship.

No wonder girls question how their Prince Charming can find them. I know that as perfect as my dad was, it was a question that weighed heavy on my mind. After all, what would bring a prince to my small town? This ordinary girl had been tucked away in her ordinary life for so long; it seemed very improbable that anyone of great importance or stature would find her. So, I worked very hard to please everyone in my path. Like Cinderella, I worked tirelessly to meet everyone's needs and follow all of the rules.

My mother had always taught me that the types of women men wanted to marry are those who are virtuous—those who are respectable. Surely my Prince Charming would hear about my

---

[1] Child Help, Inc., https://www.childhelp.org/child-abuse-statistics

goodness and start out on the quest to find me. Fortunately, God had already tugged at my heart to accept Jesus as Savior, and with every ounce of childlike faith, I did. God was my Provider, and I believed He would definitely direct my Prince Charming to me—but how?

Because my life was such a utopia, it was easy to get caught up in the Cinderella dream. In fact, it was my generation that had the lingering effects of Prince Charmings when men were raised to be men to fulfil their God-given responsibilities. Men of my generation were still being raised to respect women and treat them with dignity and honor, and women in my generation required it. Until the early '70s, very few girls gave their virtue to a man before marriage, and if they did, they were forced to marry, and finding another man who would marry them was very rare. Being good by all standards meant to follow not only biblical rules but societal rules as well. In those days, the line between the two was fairly small. There was little distinction between God and country until the '60s rebellion hit and our world spiraled into chaos.

As a young girl, the worst evil in my life was of my own making. There always seemed to be a terrible moat around my castle that was full of sea monsters. Surrounding me were hidden monsters that no one could possibly know about or understand. These personal demons tormented me day and night, and I cried myself to sleep many times, wishing that my Prince Charming would hurry up and come to my rescue before it was too late. I knew he could deliver me from my feelings of inadequacy and inferiority.

I knew my ordinary looks and ordinary ways could improve if my Prince Charming could only deliver me from my ordinary life. I believed that he could see in me what no one else was willing to see. After all, that is what my dad did.

Growing up the fourth child in a family of seven almost made me invisible. I grew up in an era when children were to be seen not heard and there was no room for expression except to God. Today's standards for children are completely the opposite. Children have the run of the house and often rule their parents. In society, children seem to be a nuisance, and adults have more leeway to act like children than the children themselves. All of this comes into play when young girls grow up and choose the men in their lives. Indulgence, permissiveness, and lack of discipline all take their toll in relationships. In my case, having a father who was enormously shy and with very little interaction created in me an innate desire to shine so bright that the right kind of man would desire me for his own.

For this reason, I remember always wanting to escape my life in utopia. From the age of four, my inferiority complexes made me feel like I was never understood or accepted. I remember packing my bag, taking my bear, and running away from home. I remember being mocked and scorned, without a thought about the insecurities being inculcated into my psyche. The truth is, I had a personality type very few people understood. Finding a way to deal with my demons was something I had to figure out on my own. Being tough was very important in that era, and if you were weak, acceptance was unobtainable.

It was easy to feel inadequate and inferior up against my siblings. All of them were pretty and intelligent, with gifts in music and popularity. I had inherited neither and believed myself less of a person because of it. I had not learned that it was not wise to compare yourself with others. Even from a toddler, I struggled with obesity and never measured up to the Twiggy body type. Popularity became very important to me as I befriended the cheerleaders and joined drill team, but for some reason, the void was still there.

Integral to my understanding of men was what I learned from my brother. Born an only son of five kids, he had his share of surviving to do. Mother constantly reiterated how very much he loved his sisters until the third one (me) was born, and then he turned on us all. Being the middle boy of four girls, it always seemed incumbent upon him to prove his masculinity. Unfortunately for us, he used us girls as stepping stones to achieve that milestone!

I can't help but pause for a moment and recognize the importance of birth order and situational circumstances in men. Kevin Leman, author of *The Birth Order Book*, gives us insight into why boys behave the way they do. Birth order has a lot to do with their attitudes, natures, and choices. Leman identifies middle children as "mysterious" and suggests that they form their person from many different directions, particularly the elder siblings. Since my brother had sisters to look up to, it became evident that there were some masculine traits that needed to shine forth. He was not about to become a *girl.*

His proudest accomplishment as an adolescent was becoming an Eagle Scout. He was at his best when faced with the challenges of the survival of the fittest. That he did particularly well in every area of life. True to the Boy Scout Oath, he seeks to do his best for God, his country, and people. He is morally straight and has developed a strong mental acumen through the study of God's Word.

During my adolescence, my brother never offered me the big brother image of fighting for my honor or beating down the bullies. He has, however, more than made up for it in my adulthood. It seemed apparent during our teen years that he was on proving ground. He was the type who would try anything once, and it seemed to always get him in more trouble than he expected. Oddly enough, his favorite book was *Tom Sawyer,* whom he set out to emulate on a regular basis.

After much prayer and intercession, though, this prodigal son soon came home; and when he arrived, what celebration! He is gifted beyond description in preaching God's Word and in compelling others to come to the Savior. He is probably best recognized for his compassion and burden for souls, which, without fail, continues to be a beacon to a hurting world. His arms have always gone out to the youth who, like him, have gone astray in choices and desires.

He is vivacious and funny and always has a story to tell that brings others to laughter. That medicine to the soul has followed him wherever he goes. Many a time, I have seen him lighten a dark situation with his bright smile or a word fitly spoken in due season. In observing him, I see many characteristics of my dad. His contagious smile and infectious laughter were God-given, and he passed it down to a generation failing in the joy of living. In days when joy was impossible for me and was nowhere in sight, my brother brought about a succoring of need that gave me hope and gladness of heart.

Having a brother or brother figure in your life brings balance to the unreasonable expectations we might place on men. When we live day in and day out with our brothers. We can see that they too have a downside. Seeing men as human always helps satiate the longing for perfection!

As I continued to look for my Prince Charming, though, many times my moat full of sea monsters grew deeper and more treacherous as I tried to be all things to all people without compromising my principles. Oddly enough, it was my boldness that became a point of admiration for many of those I tried to emulate, and eventually, my transparency became a refreshing attribute that kept me above water.

The problem remained, however, that even if my Prince Charming could find where I lived and could cross the dangerous moat, he still had to fight the fire-breathing dragon named society. Outside of my door at the very bottom of the stairwell was a dragon mightier than any enemy I could have ever conjured up. Society was mean and cruel and consumed anyone in his path. I did not please society half the time because I was too large or too small, too loud or too soft-spoken, too happy or too sad; and I certainly did not know how to play society's games. Society always made fun of me and rejected anything I could offer to win his acceptance. I never seemed to do the right thing at the right time to meet society's demands, so he decided to keep me imprisoned from all forms of happiness and fulfillment.

My developmental years both emotionally and physically were during the 1960s. For those who know its history, living in the '60s was vastly different than Hollywood's image of free love and "if it feels good, do it." Even though permissiveness was commonplace on both coasts, in heartland America, morals and civil obligations remained. While we watched the shootings at Penn State and the Watts riots on television, most Americans still sought God's favor. While protestors marched against the Vietnam War to the White House door, in the heartland, we trembled at the thought of our loved ones being drafted but prayed God's protection upon those who were called up.

Eventually, however, secular influences infiltrated even the heartland. At first, we said the Lord's Prayer and read a chapter from the Bible in public school. It was then that I was introduced to boys in a way I could hardly identify. On the way home from school, a neighbor boy kissed me. I was so embarrassed that I ran home to tell my dad and got a spanking for letting him. Thus began my idea of love between a boy and a girl. It was awkward and hurtful, but somehow, I didn't mind it.

Then, we heard the news that John Fitzgerald Kennedy had been shot. Eventually, prayers in public schools were completely abolished and the Bible was not to be a part of the school curriculum. The Bible Society set up booths thirty yards away to give Bibles to kids as they walked home from school.

Very little was said about why these changes happened, and our parents seemed oblivious to their impact. There were no political statements or commentaries made in church, and the government seemed to have exercised its stealthy power in the dead of night. No doubt there were similar milestones in American culture as you were growing up that began building your foundation of ideas about people, ethics, and what was right and wrong.

It wasn't long before I enjoyed my first steady boyfriend, and my mother was horrified. He walked me home from school every day and listened adoringly while I babbled on about anything and everything. It was a match made in heaven even to the point where he gave me his grandmother's ruby necklace as a testament to his love for me. A few days later, he made me mad and I tore it from my neck and threw it in the trash. Okay, so I had become a drama queen. What would anyone expect! Even though we went through high school together, he never forgave me.

As time would tell, shortly thereafter my neighbor across the street serenaded me one night under my bedroom window with a love song he had written just for me. Boys weren't so bad after all, but it only deepened my drive to compare them to the goodness of my dad.

During my adolescence, my neighbor and dear friend was raped in the field behind our house where we used to play. When my friend came back to school, the rumors had run rampant, and no one knew what to say to her. Eventually, her family moved away, and we never heard from her again.

Naïve to such evil, I didn't even know what it meant to be raped. I just knew it was bad and hurtful. I remember feeling so sorry for her and wanting to be there for her, but I didn't know how. Her ghostly expressions and sullen demeanor haunted me for a long time. I can only imagine how her image of men was developed from that experience.

Consider, though, the impact of today's culture where rape is a byword. Children of the youngest age have been acquainted with levels of evil we never dreamed. Imagine how their image of a good man is tainted and twisted. Even though it has subsided somewhat, approximately two-hundred seventy-three thousand teen pregnancies occur each year in the United States.[2] In the most sexually educated generation of all time, 77 percent of those pregnancies are unintended. Seven out of every ten American teenagers have engaged in sexual intercourse by their nineteenth birthday; and the abortion rate among teenagers averages 30 percent of all US abortions.[3]

---

[2] Teen Help, Inc., https://www.teenhelp.com/teen-pregnancy/teen-pregnancy-statistics
[3] Teen Pregnancies Statistics, http://www.teenpregnancystatistics.org/content/teenage-abortion-statistics.html

Society has really done a number on our current generation of girls. What idea must they have of a man? What image have they been given to espouse a healthy relationship with a man?

Then came my awkward, excruciating, agonizing, wonderful first real kiss. While playing hide-and-seek with the neighborhood kids, one of the boys I had a crush on found me in the bushes. Unbeknownst to me, he had a crush on me and asked if he could kiss me. Of course, I told him yes. He planted a peck on my lips and ran off. His ignorance of how to express love for a girl only deepened my insecurities as I tried to reconcile his actions with my ideas of what love should be. They hardly matched.

It wasn't long before the world had evolved into something no one recognized. My generation was the first to serve as the guinea pigs for the new world order. From a spiritual perspective, churches could only identify the abrupt and malevolent changes as communistic and fought the red state of communism on every political front. Parents took up the banner against communism and carried it with zeal to the end of the '70s until they realized something much graver was targeting their kids.

Little by little, layer upon layer, experiences were producing in me a montage of what a man should be—how a man should act and the pros and cons of men and their peculiar ways. To an ordinary girl, men were very complicated. It is here where many women might be struck by the notion that all men are the same. I, personally, have never met men who are the same. A lot of them have the same nature, but rest assured, every man is individually formed as God intended. It is this beauty that offers the promise of a soul mate.

If only my Prince Charming could make it through! I knew that I could make it worth his while. I would be the best wife he could ever desire. I could have his children and raise them to be the best children in the world. Nothing could stop me if only Prince Charming would get me out of the prison and torment I was experiencing. Like Cinderella, I tried to learn everything I needed to learn about winning him. There were many things I did not understand, but I was willing to do almost anything to be delivered.

It was during those years that I was introduced to a small nondenominational group of girls called Teen Ethics. Mrs. Louise Oldham saw unsuspecting teenage girls being ravaged by the deceitful tactics of a permissive culture. She established a time for girls from all faiths to gather once a month and ask any questions they might have. The answers were found in God's Word and there was never one question that the Bible couldn't answer—even about sex. In addition, Teen Ethics introduced my generation of girls to charms and social graces our parents had been too busy or frayed to instill into our lives.

I was emboldened with as many questions as there were pages in the Bible, and those meetings were never dull. If I was going to find Prince Charming, I had to know how to plan accordingly. The fact that it was consistent to God's plan solidified my focus. It was here that the perfect storm of my life came together. Even though the '60s had been turbulent nationally, in my little world, I was still able to find a force for good. That coupled with godly parents who practiced what they preached and a Bible-believing church that proclaimed God's Word as the core of all truth, I started on a spiritual journey that remains to this day.

I am hardly mentioning the ins and outs of my approach to finding men as a model. I do, however, want to provoke thought within to help us understand our selection of the men we allow into our lives. What foundations were laid in your life? What memories do you have that helped build on what to look for in men? What choices in life led you into your relationships? When in brokenness, these are the roots of our despair that need to be addressed.

Day by day, I carried out a ritual of learning everything I could get my hands on. I studied and practiced and worked hard to become accomplished and pleasing to someone of my Prince Charming's social character. I learned a lot about myself during these formative years that gave me confidence. I was able to create a "fight" within me that even made society shriek. My most treasured possession was the Book of Truth that brought me to a new understanding about myself and those around me.

For most girls my age, it was a time of self-discovery and exploration. Many of my friends were trying sex for the first time, experimenting with drugs, and exploring the tenets of different religions. I, on the other hand, had already decided what I wanted to be, how I was going to get there, and what I was going to do. I disregarded the criticisms and negativities of society and my own treacherous demons and moved forward without looking back.

Every day I searched for answers about how to find my Prince Charming from God's most precious Book. I also learned a lot about society from this Book and was able to deal with its threats and scare tactics. I could not wait to share this priceless treasure with my Prince Charming. Surely he had already learned of the Book of Truth and we could share Its wealth together. What a powerful couple we could make!

I believed with all of my heart that God had called me into fulltime ministry as a preacher's wife to serve in a church, raise a godly family, and one day administrate a Christian school. I knew that God would send my Prince Charming to not only deliver me from my prison but release me to do God's will. By now, I had developed long-lasting friendships, mainly with boys, and learned how to engage them. It was gratifying to see how boys would open up to me and tell me their woes, all the while asking me to set them up with my friends.

Surprisingly, this was also a time when my physical development had reached an impasse. I was what a lot of people called a late bloomer. Physical repercussions created devastating setbacks for me. Mother immediately took me to the doctor, who had no more an idea of how to treat me than my mother did. He began harsh experiments on my fragile body, such as high-powered steroids, reproductive surgery at the age of fifteen, and numerous birth control methods. These would be the torment of my childbearing years.

Naturally, these numerous treatments created physical ramifications that were neither accepted nor embraced by boys my age. I constantly fought sporadic weight gains, bloating, irritability, and depression. My feelings stayed on a roller coaster throughout my pubescence, and there was rarely a moment I didn't show my raw emotions. I immediately began to mask my insecurities with humor or eating, and little was done to walk me through my misery. Looking back, it is amazing how our physical bodies affect every aspect of our lives, particularly our physical attractions and concept of men.

It didn't take long to see, however, that it seemed only boys who had no interest in God were interested in me. My strengths had drawn out their weaknesses, and I became a challenge for those with wrong intentions. It appeared I was always a brass ring away from popularity.

I had developed best friendships with two girls who shared my values and commitment to virtue. One was frail because of having been born with a hole in her heart, and the other was one of few (at the time) who was from a single-parent home. We shared a deep and abiding friendship into young adulthood and helped each other deal with the emotional issues boys brought into our lives. It was a bond God gave me to guard my heart and preserve my virtue.

Still, I hoped and dreamed for my Prince Charming because I knew he would be just like Dad. After all, I had finally become a princess.

CHAPTER 2

The Fairy Princess

Being a princess isn't all it's cracked up to be.

—Princess Diana

As Cinderella grew up under the iron hand of her wicked stepmother, she maintained her work ethic and propensity to find good in everyone. Even though grave injustices had branded her path, there was always a man God put in her way to walk her through the toughest times. Male friends guided her along and were able to lend insights into her naivety.

Similarly, the men God put in my life to cultivate my image of men became a portrait of what I eventually looked for in my Prince Charming; and the same is true of any woman. I learned very quickly that *no one* could measure up to my dad, so I looked for the good in all the men that came my way.

As time wore on, I filled my days with ordinary things. I learned how to write and recite poems and develop in charms of grace and poise. I was drawn to a gracious spirit and longed to have that very special virtue. It was not my nature to be gentle and quiet. In fact, many people did not like me because of my loud and boisterous personality. Sometimes I was very uncouth and a public embarrassment to my family.

Like all females, learning how to fit into a culture that was foreign to me was difficult. There were embarrassing moments, humiliating circumstances, and excruciating lessons to learn. The world had far surpassed my street knowledge, and I became a joke to a lot of boys who couldn't help but laugh at my gullibility. The new school curriculum didn't help. The new way of being was more provocative than anything I had ever learned. After all, I had always been taught to learn sexual things from my husband.

While sitting in psychology, I remember hearing a word many today use as a byword. I had never heard of anything like that and asked the teacher to explain it. The boys in the back of the room fell out of their chairs in laughter. Having only one boy in our family who *never* showed himself in anything less than full apparel, I couldn't comprehend how boys were sexually. It was a rude awakening for me as I realized I might have become a fairy princess, but I was in no way ready for my Prince Charming.

Such naivety in today's culture is virtually obsolete. Today, girls have learned more about sexual conduct and misconduct in their formative years than I have learned in a lifetime. Sensory overload in our promiscuous society has changed girls' chemistry and physical makeup. Psychologists are telling us today that girls are facing puberty earlier and earlier because of the sexual content they have been exposed to early in life. Unfortunately, it has impeded the ability for girls to grow into sexual maturity. Instead, they are plunged into a "know all, be all" sexual object—the exact outcry of the women's movement.

Fortunately for me, however, God gave me a mentor in my sister. Being five years older than me, she was a perfect testimony to emulate even though she was prettier and much more talented. My sister and her boyfriend slowly began teaching me how boys and girls were supposed to be together. They would take me on dates with them, and we would converse about relationships. I would see him holding her hand or kissing her and enjoyed watching their romance bloom. When they fought, I watched how they reconciled and began to understand that relationships were hard.

It was my older sister's great fortune to eventually marry the man of her dreams. Much of the reason for the strength of her marriage is because of the man she chose. The youngest of six children, he came from a family whose dad believed in hard work and labor. He put his boys to work the minute they could lift a finger and never let up on them. His mother was dedicated to prayer, and her belief in God was heartily instilled in him at a young age. Even though his dad was not a practicing believer, his mom made sure her kids were in church whenever she could arrange it.

Of all the kids in their family, I see my brother-in-law as the cream of the crop. He is a jack of all trades—very astute in business, a master salesman, a prolific artist, and a superb friend. He possesses the gift of discernment and can read people instantly. His innate ability to size up a situation has developed in him the skill to recognize and know how to act in any critical situation.

Probably one of the most important steps in finding a man to share life with is to recognize the difference between being street smart and discerning. A man who is able to recognize evil and avoid it is worthy of love. A man who has the capacity to discern the thoughts and intents of the heart can protect a woman in her vulnerabilities. A man who is skilled in managing worldly situations without being worldly is someone every woman needs. That man was my brother-in-law.

I first met him in middle school. He drove up in a black '59 Ford Falcon with the back windshield out. He told me the story of how it was shattered, but we will not mention that now. I loved him from the very beginning and always encouraged my sister to keep him in the family. It was not unusual for me to bring him into the conversation after every date with another guy even when there did not seem to be much hope for them to get together. When they finally did join hearts, he generously showed me the ropes in many areas of my own attempts to find my Prince Charming and gave me solid advice in the absence of my dad.

He has the heart of a lamb and is a giant in integrity and stature. Through his own ingenuity, he has become a first-class philanthropist at whose hands this author has experienced much compassion and benevolence. It is difficult for a single parent to put into words what it means to have someone provide the monies needed when it looks like everything is going to be lost. In those perilous times, my brother-in-law came to my aid and kept me afloat when no one else would.

I had the privilege of working with him for a year and a half at his business. His work ethic and the respect held from his employees expressed the beauty of his person. Very few people have anything bad to say about him because he is always going about doing good. Even during the greatest controversy of his life, he held his head up and took the high road in achieving maximum results under dire circumstances. Much more damage could have been done to his business, his friends, his family, and his coworkers if he had not stayed by the stuff and held to his convictions.

His most virtuous adornment of his character lies in his art. He exposes a rare side of humankind and his own inner soul when he paints. One painting particularly dear to me was given to me as a baby gift just before I lost my son. It was a picture of a little boy with a baseball hat twisted to the side of his head. In that boy's eyes were the lost days of summer and the eminent return to school. Adequately titled, it is called "Summer's Over." The way he captured the heart of that child was indicative of his ability to capture the core of human nature.

His compassion for humanity has been demonstrated in his life over and over again. He has an unquenchable zest for life and lives it to its fullest. I am so grateful that he has shared that passion with me, especially at a time when I needed to know that life was worth living.

One quote he gave in a devotion was burnished into my heart as I searched for my Prince Charming:

> Strength lies between the bonding of the old and new. It is strength and wisdom for the young to look to the experience of the old and the old to look to the discoveries of the young.

In becoming the princess God intended me to be, I learned the importance of learning from all the men God put into my path. All of them influenced my idea of my Prince Charming. Like Cinderella, I armed myself with what I had learned from them. Their influence protected me along the journey, and I ventured out past the dragon and over the moat to find the man of my dreams at Cinderella's ball.

The first stop on my journey was at the home of a handsome football jock. He was immediately very eager for my company, which made me wary. No one had ever been eager for my company before, so I found myself withdrawn and hesitant to get to know him. After all, he looked like what I thought my Prince Charming should be, and he did live in a big castle. But I just couldn't be sure. Finding him was just too easy; there must be a catch. We spent a lot of time together, and before long, I completely forgot about making it to the ball.

He was popular and gregarious. He appealed to my adventurous spirit, and lucky for me, his eye was on me. For a girl who felt she had never been noticed or wanted, meeting him was a dream come true. We met on the way to church camp in Colorado. He asked me to sit with him on the bus, and we talked all the way. According to his friends, he had never opened up to anyone like he opened up to me.

Amazingly, I found my Prince Charming in him. He was strong, blond, and handsome! He had a presence of confidence that I was later to realize was not as strong on the inside as it appeared on the outside. He was a well-known varsity football player who was gifted in butting heads and blocking large human beings from getting a small pigskin ball. He was every girl's dream, and in this particular time of life, he chose me!

In spite of his gruff exterior, our time together tendered him in areas that surprised everyone. He was completely vulnerable with me, so I told him all about the Book of Truth and what it had done in my life. He readily accepted its power, which brought an even deeper understanding to our time together. During a one-week excursion at church camp, he openly shared his life's experiences and genuinely listened to mine. He quoted poems, carried me up hills, and with loving tenderness picked wildflowers from the mountainside. As love goes, I would suspect him to be my first.

Our week together was the sweetest I have ever known, and that one week out of my life time has remained as fresh today as it was fifty plus years ago. Our chemistry was like a warm fire that eventually blazed with passion. He listened to every word I said, and I couldn't wait to find out more about him. He told me about his family and how he and his dad always fought. I told him about my family and the monsters I had to fight every day just to step outside the house. He gave me a special poem, and I told him about Jesus. Eventually, he came to know Christ as his Savior, and I was sure he was the one. When the week was over, though, we went back to life as usual; and I didn't understand how boys could do that.

Men are created with the inherent ability to deduce logic and manage life's circumstances. They rarely know they have such gifts, but when put to the test, most men are naturally capable of such astuteness by setting the emotions aside. Their left-brain leanings make them pragmatic in their decisions and give them a natural resilience if they are wrong. Love, however, clouds their judgment, which is one reason they run from it with such intensity.

One day, First Love left and asked me to wait for him. Days passed and then weeks and then months before he came back. I had waited patiently, believing with all of my heart that by now I had found my Prince Charming. He would be the one to put the finishing touches on my tiara and polish my rough edges. When he returned, however, I hardly recognized him. His beautiful hair was strewn in confusion; and his handsome physique had become scarred from the many wars he had fought during our time away. His beautiful lips that used to sing forth praises about me had become snarled and twisted with harsh words and calloused insults. He had gotten entangled with society on his journey and wanted nothing to do with me. Society had told him that I was just ordinary and would never measure up to his standards. He was convinced that he could find someone much better than I could ever be.

One of the hardest lessons I had to learn was that boys and men rarely let their guard down even to those they love. It is very important that their image stay strong and manly. To love was to be weak, and to be virtuous, for a man of my generation, was begging to be ridiculed. I didn't know that boys and men could turn their emotions off like a faucet and feign love like a game.

That is exactly what happened to him. When he got home, he realized how vulnerable he had been and was not about to lose his jock image over a Christian girl who would never give in to him. He had already had his way with the girls, and no one denied him. He had come too close to losing his heart with me for him to throw it away on something that guaranteed no returns.

We only saw each other three times after our week together, but according to friends, he didn't know what to do with what he was feeling for me. During those last times together, he was cruel and blew off my acts of love and kindness. It was nothing for him to make fun of me in front of my friends and publicly humiliate me for loving him. He did everything in his power to crush every feeling we had built for one another.

Needless to say, I was devastated and decided that the journey to my Prince Charming was just too hard. When he discarded me, I was left to survive in the bitter cold. There was no one to come to my aid, and since, obviously, he was not my Prince Charming, I did not feel like there was anyone to protect me. I crawled into a nearby cave just to get out of the cold and laid my weary head down to rest.

I have found it true that a bond that is bound in the spiritual is a bond that is bound for eternity. Such was the case with us. In those glorious days, he met the Lord as His Savior, and it solidified all that we had already shared. But he had to phase back into the jockdom of his high school, and he would never again share such vulnerability.

While I was standing in the kitchen one day, my mother called his name and asked me if I knew him. I told her yes, and she said he had been killed in a car wreck. He was coming home from a camping trip in Arizona and was riding in the back of a pickup truck driven by a fifteen-year-old. Being an inexperienced driver, the boy hit the shoulder of the road and lost control, causing the pickup to roll several times. My first love was crushed and died instantly.

I went into immediate shock when Mother told me the news. Of course, she knew nothing of our history. The words were still hanging in the air when I barreled out of the front door and ran as fast as I could down the street, screaming and crying. To say the least, I had an emotional breakdown that no one could understand. How could one week with a guy have such a huge impact on my life?

At the viewing, they had to pull me away from the casket. I couldn't take my eyes off of him and wondered whether I had entered his mind at all since we had spoken our last words. He had consumed my thoughts, and knowing he didn't give me a second thought was too much to bear. I was weak sitting through the funeral and remember thinking my world had come to an end. I couldn't think of anything being said but was totally consumed by our last words, which were cruel and heartless. I spent years contacting friends and acquaintances, trying to find out what he said before he died. I just couldn't believe he meant what he said.

The news came very hard to me; after all, he really could have been my Prince Charming. I longed to bring closure to our harsh words and horrible ending, so when there was no answer, I turned to the Book of Truth. It taught me that I could bring my own closure to the circumstances of life, which are forever left open even though it would take me a lifetime to learn it. I learned to cherish our memories together and whispered a prayer of gratitude for all he had taught me along my journey. He made me the princess I had become.

We always hear about the impact first loves have on our lives. How many times have we heard that we never get over our first love and how we always build on our first love? In my life, that has been true. Unfortunately, there was no closure for me at that time. Our last words cut into my soul and scarred my capacity to love. To know gentleness, adoration, vulnerability, and unadulterated love for a solid week *and* to be tied with a spiritual bond is hard to beat. It would permanently impair my ability to understand, know, or even embrace love again.

That coupled with rejection and abandonment does not make for a good future in love. Months after his death, I just could not get back. My mother was so worried that she sent me to California for three weeks to stay with my former youth directors. It was really a coming-of-age experience for me as I saw a whole new world I had never experienced. California was beautiful, but the people there were very loose and unassuming. Grown men would hit on me, and what I wore and how I talked became a constant object of ridicule. It was interesting to see how I gained more attention than I needed or wanted during that time. If I had been mentally healthy, I probably would have relished it, but all that trip did was numb my soul.

Because of my experience with First Love, I learned to never minimize the seemingly insignificant griefs that came the way of the youth with whom I worked for twenty years. What a lesson he gave me in his short life: that boys do turn to men and that words quickly spoken in regret truly do make an imprint on others for the rest of their lives. I learned the importance of keeping perspective and to balance a boy's harsh words against an unforgettable week of gentle kindness and love. I can only conclude that that week revealed his true self.

> Though nothing can bring back the hour
> Of splendor in the grass, of glory in the flower;
> We will grieve not; rather find strength in what remains behind;
> In the primal sympathy which having been must ever be;
> In the soothing thoughts that spring out of human suffering;
> In the faith that looks through death, in years
> that brings the philosophic mind.
>
> —William Wordsworth

To put my shattered heart back together again, God put a man in my life named Comfort to grow me in my journey and develop in me a deeper perspective of men. He was four years older than me and full of life and personality. He had a unique way of making me laugh and met my every insecurity head on. He encouraged me, cared for me, and reached out to me. He introduced me to a mature relationship that didn't harbor ill will or insecurities. He sheltered my naivety and appreciated it. It wasn't humorous or immature to him; in fact, to him, it was virtuous. He taught me more about men and gave me insights into what a real man should be. He cherished me and sheltered me in the midst of the cruelest rejection I had ever known. When he was confident that I was okay, Comfort was gone.

I couldn't help but believe that my Prince Charming had come and gone. Many people believe that God intends for us to find only one soul mate in our lifetimes. Whether we find him or her or not tells the story of the rest of our lives. Perhaps that was true for me since I have never known a love like that since. It did not, however, stop me from trying to find a love that could compare to all of the great attributes of the men God had already put in my life.

There was one man-boy who was genuine and resurrected my love for some time. I'm sure we've all had a man like him in our lives. You know, the boy next door who seemed like such a nerd when we were growing up. He wasn't quite in the "in crowd" and certainly did not have the decorum of a jock or class favorite. One thing unique to this particular man, however, was his authenticity. It never occurred to him to be anyone but himself in his walk, his talk, his manners, or his beliefs. He was a man's man without reservation and proud of it.

Even though we had grown up together since birth, I'll never forget the first real encounter I had with him. He and his friends were the typical boys who acted their age. They were the type who would dip girls' pigtails in ink wells or throw spitballs in class. Ordinary though he seemed, he was made of all the right stuff; and I confess today that he was the one that got away. Like Cinderella, I threw apples at my prince without even knowing who he was.

It wasn't until my birthday that I suspected he remotely cared for me. Juvenile as it seems, his friends bound him up and forced him to give me my first birthday kiss. It never occurred to me how difficult that was for him. We volleyed our affection for one another over the years from hate to love to love-hate. He even asked me to go on a date and insisted that we go Dutch! What was I thinking?

I finally realized that with all his idiosyncrasies, this one was a keeper. Every woman wants a man who will allow himself to get vulnerable with her without sacrificing his manhood in the process. That was him. On a cool November night, he shared with me that I had been his first love and that I had the dubious honor of being the only girl who had ever brought him to tears.

It is as if it were yesterday. My heart throbbed within me as I expressed my feelings for him, which were too late. What I didn't realize was that he could easily expose that vulnerability because he had found his true love. It was a closure I have regretted all of my life. The unassuming frog now turned Prince Charming had slipped through my fingers. How in the world did I let it happen?

I guess we could chalk this one up to immaturity—maybe timing, maybe ignorance, maybe … but when I think about it, it is clear that I just did not see the man in him. How many times have women made that mistake in their lives and like me, lived to regret it? I wonder how many women have married a Prince Charming and can't see the greatness in him. It has happened probably more times than we would care to admit. An even greater mistake than letting them go, however, is forgetting that they exist.

Gentle yet harsh, loving yet hateful, forceful yet yielding—he was and is a leader in his own right. He has followed in the footsteps of his father as a wonderful family man, and his legacy is that he was and is real—genuine in the first degree. He gave me the greatest gift of all—he taught me how to love again and most of all, how to express that love in the most difficult of circumstances. It was this love that I used as a barometer in all of my future dealings with men.

Just like Cinderella, despite my own failings with men, God still placed men in my life to protect me and shelter my naivety. When my dad died, very few men in my life could replace him. Naïve and young, I still believed there was some man somewhere who was gentle and kind, loving and faithful. As I walked that grief journey, there was a man *consistently* there to catch me when I fell—my preacher! His favorite saying was, "Consistency thou art a jewel," and his favorite Scripture was Romans 8:28.

Born on a farm in West Texas, he was a tall, strong, John Wayne type whose presence was known the minute he walked into a room. I'll never forget how he told me about my father's death. He personally looked me up on my college campus and walked me to his office with his arm around me in total comfort. I have to admit that I didn't know what was up. I had skipped class that morning, and since he was the president of the college, I was sure this little walk wasn't going to end well. Never in my wildest dreams did I suspect where that walk would lead. Waiting in his office were my older brother and sisters, all of them crying. They let me know that Dad had had a heart attack in California and that he would be coming home soon in a flag-draped coffin.

My preacher provided calm assurance to help us in any way he could. It wasn't until years later that I realized how great the loss of my father was for him. Unbeknown to us, he grieved privately at the loss of his devoted deacon and became a bastion of strength and support for a family that did not have the faintest idea what to do without a father.

As I look back over the years, that's how my preacher was. He, too, was somewhat shy and circumspect yet could boldly proclaim the Gospel of Jesus Christ without reservation. He had a brilliant mind and could administrate any kind of situation placed before him. Borne about by his love for the Lord and a burden to carry God's work forward, he spent twenty-five years of his life presiding over a Bible college and forty-five years pastoring our church.

Preacher had a zest for life that could not be squelched. It always appeared that he could not fit enough hours in the day to do all he wanted to do. His productive spirit and passion to achieve brought about the completion of an entire college campus encompassing a total of seven buildings and the erection of a complex for our church valued at several million dollars. He was the silent donor of ill-fated students, parishioners, and loved ones and provided deliverance for many who would never know how to appreciate his sacrificial gifts.

Preacher's staunch belief in the Word of God established for us all a foundation that has brought us certainty in times of uncertainty. He epitomized leadership in both stature and wisdom and walked with God as confirmation to his calling. In addition to his touch on the outside world, Preacher touched my life immensely. His door *always* remained opened to me from my silly girlhood days to the day he died.

He not only buried my father and passed his courage on to me and my family, but he also officiated my wedding and was there for the birth of my first child and the death of my second. At a moment's notice, he was there to meet the needs of this girl who looked to him as her father in the absence of her own.

Even when his health was failing, Preacher sacrificed valuable rest to meet my need during my darkest hours, all the while refusing to show his pain. When many were criticizing him and seeking to destroy his work, he stood firm and unflinching in his stand for truth. Regardless of the consequences, compromise was not a word in his vocabulary when it came to principle and integrity. With all of his successes, he never sought fortune or notoriety. Having received an honorary doctorate and numerous awards from institutes all over the country, his greatest honor was that of being called Preacher. That was where his heart was.

At his funeral, he was heralded as a man who stood in the gap and was a faithful friend to the end. Without question, he was my mentor and supporter throughout my lifetime, and his absence has left an indescribable emptiness. As they rolled his casket out of the auditorium surrounded by those who loved him, the void was clearly felt, and the cries attested to the loss of a man after God's own heart.

As his favorite Scripture says in Romans 8:28, all things have worked together for good for him because he was called according to God's purpose, and he certainly loved God without reservation. True to life, however, he also fulfilled the verse following Romans

8:28, which says, "For whom he did foreknow, he also did predestinate to be conformed to the image of His Son, that he might be the firstborn among many brethren."

No truer words were ever spoken of a simple, loving man who was predestined to give his life for his Savior and died in all of the eloquence of pure virtue. He was a genuine picture of conformity to the image of Jesus Christ not only to me but to the world he touched. Everyone who knew him was better for having the privilege of sharing life with him. As I watched his life, I formulated exactly what to look for in a man. How could any Prince Charming ever live up to that?

Becoming a princess entails the matriculation of all three aspects of a person—mind, body, and soul. Having long since climbed the hill of age, it occurs to me more than ever that being a princess begins and ends with those men who influenced us spiritually. Great neglect has come to the adornment of many women because they have failed to inculcate the spiritual into their lives. The one thing we as women seem to disregard the most is feeding and maturing our spirits. Remembering the influence spiritual men have had in our lives can resurrect the inner beauty within us that makes our crowns shine.

Because of the influence the men in my life had on me, I constantly tried to overcome my boisterous nature by surrounding myself with cultured, gracious people. I hoped that maybe they would rub off on me so I could be admired and accepted as a princess. I worked hard at learning manners that society would accept, but there always seemed to be something wrong. As time wore on, I tried to turn myself into a more polished princess so that when Prince Charming came, he would love me unconditionally. The last thing I wanted to do was embarrass him with my backward ways!

With all of my attempts and hard knocks of life, the only place I really seemed to fit in was at church. The boys there seemed to like me, and we had a lot in common; but there were so many things inhibiting those relationships. They were good boys and a lot of fun, but it was just too hard to give my heart to them. It must have been chemistry, I guess. We are dear friends even to this day, but I had a completely different idea of what my Prince Charming should be. None of those boys were interested in ministry or, really, even in church. In the end, I realized God had put them in my life as another guard of protection for me along my journey.

Just when I thought I had achieved everything necessary to be a beautiful princess, society breathed another stream of fire from its nostrils, making me think I had not achieved anything at all. I knew my Prince Charming would want me to be successful, so I worked tirelessly on developing skill sets that were acceptable. I studied and learned from all of the books I could find and sat at the feet of many successful people hoping to learn how to achieve success.

Without realizing it, I had become an administrator. My focus on seeking the Prince Charming God wanted for me and preparing for ministry kept me vigilant in honing my skills to meet the demands of such aspirations. I discovered my love for writing and became a voracious reader of self-help books. I started developing a back-up plan to support my minister husband just in case; and of course, I established a foundation of learning to administrate a Christian school.

When I started putting into practice all that I had learned, however, success seemed to escape me just like the popularity I earnestly sought during my adolescence. Its elusive nature bewildered me, and I didn't understand why I couldn't win. I knew that I had tamed society enough to get by, and I certainly had become as gracious and quiet as my personality would allow. I had good manners and was always polite. I had become quite a conversationalist and found that I was able to talk to any stranger with ease. I had even developed friendships with important people. What was wrong?

It soon became apparent that my idea of success was somewhat warped. To me, success meant to be popular, loved, and admired. So far, I just didn't see it. I had acquired a job and was walking in popular circles, even though on the fringe. I had my church friends and relished our time together, but there was hardly any time to reach the pinnacle of success to secure my Prince Charming.

Why was success eluding me? Just when I thought it was around the corner, it would run away again and again. It seemed that I was never good enough or strong enough and would not have enough money or time or connections. It was exhausting never being able to live up to others' standards. To help me through the days, I again turned to the Book of Truth more and more. It had always given me the answers when I needed them, and the more I searched for its wisdom and understanding, the more I realized that finding my Prince Charming was a journey. I knew that I had become a princess, and when I finally saw him face-to-face, he would be very pleased.

I busied myself with more and more "fillers" to being the most beautiful, the most popular, the most a Prince Charming could want. As I grew in maturity on my journey, I also grew spiritually. God continually established priorities in my life. My ideas of success soon morphed into an eternal perspective that could have only come from God's Word. As the world became more and more distant, those relationships I cherished the most were found in Christian friendships and acquaintances. Before long, I knew God was redirecting my path.

It was during those curious days that I was given a beautiful gown and very unique glass slippers by my loving pastor's wife. No one had seen in me what she had seen. She loved me as if I were her own and opened my eyes to many beautiful truths about myself that I had never before heard. One day, after many years of mentoring, I realized that God used her to adorn me with a beautiful gown of purity. She had diligently taught me the power of virtue and showed me the beauty of holiness. To make my wardrobe complete for my journey, God continued to use her to shod my feet with the clear, glassy Gospel of peace. My Prince

Charming would have to love me after seeing my beautiful gown and matching slippers.

What gown have you worn to meet your beloved? Figuratively speaking, we have all been adorned in something to win the hearts of those we have loved. Did it wear out after the first time, or was your adornment lasting and true? Were there matching accessories to your first impressions, or did you send a mixed message in your appearance? We may not think our adornments matter, but as life goes on, it is easy to realize how deceptive or manipulative we can be with our appearances.

Even though most of my friends had experimented in the sexual revolution of the '60s and '70s, it wasn't embarrassing for me to confess I was a virgin. In fact, being a virgin was still an admirable quality for most girls in heartland America. Society was halfway between respecting virtue and despising it. Raised to know better, I sat at the feet of wise, virtuous women who extolled the virtues of purity both physically and spiritually. I was challenged to stay pure regardless of the consequences and was assured a virtuous wife was what men truly desired. Day by day my journey to meet my Prince Charming became more and more lonely. So-called friends threw me to the side as they pursued different lifestyles.

I felt misunderstood and alone as even church friends saw the dichotomy of my walk and my desires. I had been living on the edge, wanting both the world's favor and God's blessing. It took several heartaches for me to understand how that was impossible. Jesus told His disciples not to marvel when the world hates you. It was difficult for me to understand that principle when the world had embraced me with open arms and had come to know me as honorable. Little did I know what they were saying behind my back.

Jesus was right. The world can never endear itself to God's people. The chasm is too wide. The greatest mistake Christians make is in thinking there is no chasm, and they are surprised when they fall in a fixed gulf of spiritual darkness. God spared me from taking that tumble, but I was very close. He protected me in many ways, but there was always a pseudo-Prince Charming out there who was a wolf in sheep's clothing.

Maybe the answer for my success was going to be at the Cinderella ball.

CHAPTER 3

The Cinderella Ball

Cinderella didn't settle for just going to
the ball; she wanted to dance!

The many male friends that Cinderella met along her way eased
her journey in obscurity and loneliness. One of her dearest friends,
Gustave, guarded her secrets and improved her self-image as she
struggled to find her way. In fact, it was Gustave who finally led
her to the Cinderella ball. Maurice protected and defended her to
ensure her safety. Leonardo gave her tools to reveal her beauty and
finally have the courage to rise above her circumstances.

So is the case with every woman. What men has God put in your
life to teach you the attributes to look for (or not to look for) in
your Prince Charming?

For me, it was clear that I could not stay trapped in my world all
my life and wait for my Prince Charming. There did not seem
to be *any* Prince Charming willing to care about my goodness

enough to cross the dangerous moat to destroy the demons hidden below and slay the dragon to rescue me. So, as the saying goes, "If the mountain won't come to Mohammed, Mohammed must go to the mountain." I had been told that I had to go to the Cinderella ball and "put myself out there" to find Prince Charming.

While my circumstances might be different than others', there is probably a time in every woman's life that we feel we have to take matters into our own hands. We grew up believing no one was going to take care of us but ourselves, so we had to pull ourselves up by the bootstraps and make it happen. I discovered in a very real way that that was a dangerous position to be in. That philosophy may be true of success in business or society or even career choices, but it can easily backfire when applied to relationships.

The stops I had already made along the way to the Cinderella ball had not gone well. They were stops that I had not anticipated. Still, there was more to experience before I entered the inner court of the castle. The next detour on my journey was very different than the first. I came across a tavern that was full of laughter and music. My spirit was refreshed by the jovial atmosphere, and there were many people who welcomed me with open arms.

Immediately, a young man came over to ask me to dance. I had grown weary of fighting through the hard knocks of my journey and was ready for some fun in my life. The young man had beautiful green eyes that pierced through my very soul. He gazed at me in adoration and even fumbled around, trying to find the beat of our song.

Green Eyes was a year older than me. He was popular and accepted in all of the notable circles. He was unpolished and uncouth but adorable in many ways. He had seen me from afar and wanted to meet me. It was flattering to know that of all the girls he could have gotten, he wanted to go out with me. He awkwardly had a friend introduce us, and we enjoyed a romantic first date.

Before long, we had our own song and walked into a beautiful garden of love. It was very easy for me to let my guard down and throw caution to the wind as I lived under his protection. The sparkle in his green eyes showed his affirmation of me in ways I had not known in a long time; and even though I knew he was not my Prince Charming, I was happy and satisfied with what we shared. He was certainly someone I enjoyed; but my willingness to settle for him made my heart sting as I thought of living out my life with him.

Green Eyes was a bad boy on many levels. It was my first introduction to a truly worldly boy who was as far from virtuous as any I had ever known. He was constantly reeling himself in from doing all of the things around me that he had grown accustomed to doing around other girls. His foul mouth and dirty antics were a forerunner to the turns our relationship would take over the next four years. Around me, he tried to be an angel, but whispers of his drinking and drugging soon came to light. He was the type who would try anything once, and he was far from a virgin.

One thing that particularly bothered me about Green Eyes was his refusal to believe the Book of Truth that had become such an intricate part of my life. That should have been my first warning sign that he was not my Prince Charming, but I still let our relationship continue. I tried every way I knew to help him understand the gold mines there, but he just refused to listen.

Eventually, the gap about our beliefs became too wide, and our affections simply could not cross over the huge abyss our differences had created. I was having so much fun I refused to give up on the possibility of finding someone to stand in the gap to bridge our feelings for each another.

My heart had grown cold after First Love's death, and I longed for love. Green Eyes had already whispered his love for me, but I just couldn't return it. I remember wishing I could love him and even asked God to give me a love for him. After all, there were so few who had ever expressed their love for me. There was a sense of desperation in my prayer as the chill of loneliness left me cold. Finally, after a while, my heart burned for him, and God had answered my prayer. Surprisingly, God had given me a love for an unlovely man. He must have wanted me to understand His love for humankind.

Having ministered to many women in my lifetime, this one issue stands out more than any other. How many women have relinquished everything (including their belief system) to be loved? Women who love the Lord usually want a man to be their spiritual leader and take charge of the home spiritually. To forfeit that only brings despair and unhappiness. Too many times women go into a relationship believing they can change their man in the spiritual realm, only to realize that God alone can accomplish such a miracle.

Green Eyes and I broke up many times but always seemed to come back together. I encouraged him to come to church and meet those who shared my passion for the Lord; and every now and then, he would come. Finally, he supposedly accepted the Lord Jesus Christ as his Savior; and I believed perhaps God was going to perform a miracle for us. My dad gave him a beautifully inscribed Bible, and my dreams of what we could be together grew stronger. It always bothered him, though, that I refused to give in to his sexual advances, and it eventually became too much for him.

He had already made plans for separation. It was not long before he asked another into his arms, and once again, I fell sick to love's cruelty. I stayed in the tavern to recuperate, and many people tended to my broken heart. They brought me soup for my soul, laughter in my despair, and support in my loneliness, but nothing seemed to take away the pain of my open wound. I learned that love is never wasted because loving is the nucleus of human life. But love can fall wasted on the wrong person.

He was cruel in his abandonment. He knew I had fallen for him, and he took advantage of humiliating me in front of his friends. He constantly stationed himself and his new girlfriend where I could see what I was missing. I remember crying uncontrollably for weeks. He taunted me with invitations and setups with other guys, but nothing was so grievous as when he called and asked to come see me. He told me he still loved me but couldn't let his girlfriend go because she wouldn't tell him no. He asked if he could see me behind her back.

The lesson I learned about true love with him was to recognize a counterfeit when it was obvious. He no more knew what love was than a snake. He had not acquainted himself with the Author of Love and never cared to learn lessons of love from Him. I was desperate to feel loved and accepted, and it made me almost accept his proposition, but I ended up giving him an ultimatum—her or me. He chose her and left me a note saying, "I will miss you. Have fun in church." Of all loves, this one showed me that when I took the fire of an ungodly man into my bosom, there would be no other alternative but to get burned.

Comfort, however, always came to my rescue. He hovered over me like a loving caregiver and was very attentive. We went out every weekend, and he stuck close by me at every social event at church. As I felt my heart plummeting once again, I stopped in midair and refused to let it fall again. The sheer mental discipline of refusing to love is the strongest of all disciplines but the most futile. His embrace and gentle caress gave me the comfort I needed during a difficult time of my life, but I could not hurt so deeply again by falling for him. I knew he would disappear as before, and it would be impossible for me to bear another rejection.

I was right. As Comfort saw me heal, he felt more and more at ease about leaving me alone. His attentions waned, and he went about living his life again without me. After a couple of years, he moved to California and made his home there. When his dad died, he came home for the funeral. My heart warmed with his delight when I saw him for the last time. As he gathered around the family kitchen that day, he told my youth director he had been in love with me all of those years. My heart broke when I heard he died of a heart attack at the young age of forty-nine.

I know it was a while in coming, but I realized from my relationship with Comfort that timing was very important in forming strong relationships. Some people are gifted with natural timing, and some are not. For those who are not gifted in this area, it is best to stay true to what you know is right. If Comfort and I had remotely discussed our affections for one another, our lives might have turned out differently. Being honest and transparent in a relationship can sometimes do more harm than good but will result in a clear conscience. Deception and manipulation, however, will come back to haunt us.

In the early '70s, the Cinderella syndrome was finishing its course. Mine was the last generation that thought all women couldn't function unless they were married and had children. Three of my girlfriends were already engaged to be married, and I had been branded as the bridesmaid and not the bride. With fear in my heart and no real prospects for the future, I scooped up the only Prince Charming I could find that by most standards met my criteria.

To my surprise, there was a boy who had his sights set on marrying me ever since I had met him. He was well known throughout the church and knew that my only desire was to be a good preacher's wife and a mother. He had every intention of being my Prince Charming from the moment he had heard. He began immediately weaving a web of deceit to draw me out of my cottage because he knew he did not have the courage to fight the battles necessary to rescue me.

Wolf was a year older and had acquired quite a reputation of virtue and chivalry. He was a favorite in our youth department, was the darling of our youth directors, and had his sights on me. After years of torture in the relationship department, I thought it best to acquiesce to someone who had shown love to me consistently for several years. What I had not learned was that love doesn't necessarily translate into determination.

Wolf began heralding all of his virtues by way of outer beauty and good works, making sure the news reached me at every turn. In the meantime, he carefully took advantage of every pitfall on my journey so that I would be drawn to the image of who he was supposed to be. As he intricately learned my strengths and weaknesses, he studied my every move and indirectly intervened into my life's circumstances without my knowledge. He had unabashedly eaten the forbidden fruit of evil and learned how to manipulate with the highest level of control.

Even though I wasn't attracted to him, I did appreciate his apparent virtue and commitment to the Lord. Most importantly, he was going to be a preacher, which would afford me the opportunity to fulfill my calling. I felt I could learn to love anyone who loved the Lord that way. As I slowly let him creep into my life, it became easy to be loved by him. He lavished me with goodness, and his family took me in like I was their own. Suddenly, I was on the other side of the spectrum. Where most women loved men who were not spiritual, I did not love a man who supposedly was.

It wasn't long before I began to doubt my own ability to recognize my Prince Charming. Wolf was everything I thought I wanted in a man, and my leanings seemed to be met with approval from everyone who mattered to me. Little did I know that no one really approved of him, and I walked down the aisle, accepting a wolf in sheep's clothing. The disparity between us was so clear that I was the only one left blindsided.

A fairy-tale marriage does not include lies and deception. For thirteen years, sorrows too sad to mention dispelled every idea I had of a Prince Charming. In His sovereignty, however, God gave me my little girl to steer me back on path just before the marriage ended. Being so adamantly opposed to divorce, I would never have left him if it hadn't been for her safety and mental well-being.

I began to think that if my journey was going to be this difficult, maybe I didn't need a Prince Charming. After all, he should be finding me! It should not be the other way around. As I recuperated from my terrible ordeal, I picked myself up and found I was a little bit stronger for the journey. I knew I should at least have a plan to protect myself from such an onslaught of deception should it ever happen again.

God was always a step ahead by introducing me to men who could show me insights into what good men were. He gingerly put me in a place of employment where males dominated the industry. Vince Lombardi once said, "Leaders are made, they are not born. They are made by hard effort, which is the price which all of us must pay to achieve any goal that is worthwhile." The vice president I assisted was just such a leader.

We've probably all had an all-American in our lives, maybe not in the sense of a proper title or a sports figure but they've permeated our lives with positive motivation and aggressive appeal. I am sure that in identifying everybody's all-American, they would be seen as that jock in high school who remained forever sports-minded. Exercise freak is probably an understatement for these types of men, and of course, virtues like loyalty and commitment are a given.

The name of their game is winning, and failure is not an option. If mistakes occur, which are allowable to a small degree, it is incumbent upon us to learn by them and never make them again. They believe in Mom, baseball, and apple pie and find their drive in the spirit to achieve. They are the men's men of this century and hold a distinct reflection of our culture.

When God put him in my life, he epitomized everybody's all-American. He was a motivating factor in many of my professional successes, and he and his family were a mainstay for my daughter and me through her teenage years. He is committed to his wife of over forty years and strives to bring about the continual success of his children.

He can conceivably be identified as the salt of the earth. He comes from a family that held to the old-fashioned ideas of respecting your parents and helping your neighbor. He can be called upon at any time to come to the aid of a friend or loved one; and if he is not available, he is just resourceful enough not only to find someone who can come to their aid but motivate them to do it. His timing is impeccable, and his insights are sure and solid. His favorite motto is to work hard so he can play hard, and that he does. Rest to him is putting in eighteen holes of golf and then staying up half the night hashing over the hits and misses of the game with his teammates. Any sport is a part of his vernacular, and he is challenged by new sports with which he is not familiar.

In business, he drives his people hard and rewards them handsomely. It is not in his nature to accept anything less than strong business ethics or superior results even though he may be willing to fudge in accomplishing those things for his people. Competition (healthy or unhealthy) is his motivator, and without exception, he will have a quote or cliché that justifies any game plan he may have to *win*. He could not care less about what people think because in his mind, they should be thinking his way or they need to come around!

Throughout my career, some of our company's most successful programs and strongest volume builders were a direct result of his work. He believes strongly in the team spirit. He recognizes that he cannot do it alone, and it is not unusual for him to attribute the pinnacle of his success to others.

It has often been said that the greatest leaders are those who know how to surround themselves with the greatest people. Without question, his gift is recognizing talent and giving full liberty for those talents to be exhausted in superior effort. His willingness to let his employees be free to be created one of the most solid departments in our company. His department held the highest tenure and brought about the strongest numbers in leadership skills and productivity.

His roots run deeper than a scoreboard or the numbers in a game; they reach down to the very core of the American spirit. It is that beautiful attribute that inspires us all, and I am sorry to see them diminish in American society for the sake of the almighty dollar. I am so grateful to have been a part of his life in the corporate world, and I learned from him the hope of a future.

As I made my way to the Cinderella ball, I learned alternatives to being a "help-meet" to men in my life. I was an executive assistant for some of the greatest men in the industry. I know that jokes go around about the wife at work, but God designed women to complement weaknesses. Being in a male-dominated industry gave me opportunity to fulfill my design and bring my strengths to the table. With each venture, I grew in understanding and development, particularly in working with men.

I began to understand that men were molding and shaping my life even if they weren't my Prince Charming. Their impact, whether as a supervisor, brother, friend, relative, or even men I had fallen for, were a stepping stone to accepting the Prince Charming God had planned for me. Line upon line, precept upon precept, man by man, I was learning the makeup of the male species.

Another man God graciously put into my life served as vice president in another department. He believed that he could get everything out of life he wanted just by helping other people get what they wanted. That has been the mainstay of our friendship all of these years. Known throughout today's business world is the enviable position of the world's most successful salesman. His portfolio would include a notable list of Fortune 500 companies, an impressive itinerary of network clientele, and a dancing pitch that could sell Noriega on prison. That describes him perfectly. He is the best salesman I have ever met.

Of course, always in question with salesmen is their integrity and truthfulness. A smile comes to my heart when I think of how a salesman can skillfully use manipulative strategies to close a deal. We have had this conversation many times trying to determine that fine line between honest sales tactics and deceitful manipulation. We've both concluded that the line is drawn in the sand by God Himself and is measured out in motive.

He has not been without his mistakes, but he does thrive on taking the position for integrity and right. In many instances, I have seen him take stands not only against his peers but also his supervisors that have jeopardized his position and sales standing. Particularly close to my heart is the faith we share in a Lord who guides us by the integrity of His own heart even though we live in a world that will make a sale at any cost. The affinity we harbor for one another is strong and deep. We are kindred spirits that can finish each other's sentences and encapsulate each other's thoughts. Ours has been one of the greatest partnerships I have ever known in the working world.

He literally grew up under the leadership of our company's chairman. At the ripe old age of eighteen, he joined the company at the bottom and worked his way up to vice president. He is now owner of one of the most successful distributorships in the system. He seeks to maintain the company philosophy to "treat others as you would want to be treated," which serves as a beacon to a business world that lauds profitability as primary and foremost. There has been a lot of transition over the years in that company, and it seems that in concentrating on the bottom line that mission statement got lost in the shuffle. His leadership has been instrumental in keeping the principles alive that were initiated by the Chairman.

He is a devoted family man and has endured heavy adversity in his life. Having come from the pains of a broken home, he was the man of the house for most of his teenage life. He struggled to help his mother raise his sisters and brother, and he has secured a strong and loving relationship with them. He weathered a difficult first marriage that resulted in divorce and left him serving as father and mother to his firstborn son. He later found the girl of his dreams and is now the proud father and grandfather of two.

He is a natural with people, and his diplomatic appeal and smooth ways endear people to him immediately. Of all the things in his life, the most important are the relationships he has established over the years. Friendships are very dear to him and he is committed to them, many times at his own personal risk. I have been blessed to know him and have worked with him in several business endeavors. It has been my privilege to call him friend and see how God has blessed his life. God uses him to continue to rebuild those foundational principles we have seen lost in corporate America.

It is through my relationship with him that I have been able to trust my intuition. I have mostly ignored my intuition all of my life because I didn't trust it. Many mistakes along my path have been made because I didn't listen to my innermost judgment. God gives women a particular gift in intuition that should never be ignored. When tempered with God's Word, a woman's intuition can stop wars, divert catastrophes, and influence the lives they touch. Just think about how Pilate's life would have been changed if he had listened to his wife's intuition!

I learned to never take for granted those men God has put in my path—young or old, good or bad, spiritual or not. They touch our lives just as much as we touch theirs. To dismiss their impact in grooming us to be a princess is a mistake.

Halfway through my journey to the Cinderella ball, God introduced me to a loyal scribe. Very rarely in the course of a lifetime does a common, law-abiding citizen have the need for a lawyer. It was not until I was divorced that I was even familiarized with an attorney; and for obvious reasons, it wasn't a very pleasant experience. Ironically, or should I say providentially, when I joined the company I was with for almost thirty years, I was to be a legal assistant to our general counsel. I had never been in a legal environment before and was certainly in for a rude awakening when dealing with those in the legal field. By generic descriptions, lawyers are "different" animals. They have a personality and genre all their own, and believe me, it was not one that fit my personality and quirks!

One can only imagine, then, why it was surprising that I worked so well with this attorney. He is a staunch Christian believer with seven of the loveliest children you could ever meet. He is totally *family* and is solely committed to his wife. It was his loving patience and solid focus that ended up taking me through some of the worst years of my adult life.

Shortly after we began working together, my ex-husband filed a custody suit that nearly broke me in half financially and emotionally. Unlike myself, he had remarried and had full support during this ordeal. I, on the other hand, was forced to attend mediations and legal proceedings alone and was completely naïve to their motive.

It was during this time that this faithful scribe supported me both as a loving friend and as a loyal employer. His understanding and patience transcended my own grief and turmoil and gave me solid ground to stand upon. Precipitating the whole ordeal was my daughter's need for therapy. She had begun having nightmares, was emotionally riddled, and was showing signs of some deep issues with which I was not ready to deal. He was there for me through it all, offering stable advice as I rode my emotional roller coaster almost to a nervous breakdown.

Any parent will acknowledge that nothing goes deeper than someone's help and support when your kids are at risk. He literally walked me through the valley of the shadow of death, and I will eternally be grateful to him. His faith in God's sovereignty never wavered, and his commitment to what was right never faltered even when I wanted to take justice into my own hands. He provided me with financial, legal, and emotional resources I would never have otherwise had and showed me in every way what being a Christian man was all about.

We have since parted ways as employer/employee, and I have watched his own faith be put to the test since those grueling days gone by. He remains a bulwark of everything I believe in, and his delight in God's law has come shining through. By knowing him, I can't help but think of those scribes of old who so meticulously wrote and studied the precious Law of God. No wonder they were willing to risk life and limb for its publication! If any of them had the heart of this man, it isn't hard to understand why!

With each male friendship God gave me, new measurements lined the way in knowing what I needed in my Prince Charming. As a princess, learning friendly characteristics in men before finding a prince was a very different concept. I never knew about how to develop relationships with men, and going to a Cinderella ball seemed to be the only way I could apply all that I had learned. The Book of Truth had never alluded to a ball. Certainly, society had never before mentioned to me that I needed to "put myself out there." In fact, the opposite was true. Until now, my family, society, and even the Book of Truth indicated that the only way my Prince Charming could ever be found was for him to rescue me, but I grew tired of waiting. Oh, if women only knew the importance of what transpires when we wait!

I was becoming a woman, and life was passing me by. I wanted to have fun and enjoy life. My independent nature came out in full force, and for someone who had never tried or done anything "bad," it was time for me to push the envelope and get out there. I was still naïve to the dangers of trying to hold hands with God and the world at the same time. Men began responding to me, and finally, I was on their radar.

To my surprise, I got excited about the journey of finding my true Prince Charming. It seemed like an adventure full of fun and daring. By now, it was a breeze for me to slip by society without waking him, glide over the moat without disturbing my demons, and no one would care or be troubled by my leaving. Finally, there I stood looking down the road to the castle. Would this be it? Would I finally find someone because I made myself available in this way? Off I went with my beautiful gown (a little worse for wear) and glass slippers. Into the unknown I ran with passions flaring for love and romance.

It wasn't very long before my passions came full circle. I knew exactly what I wanted and how to get it, but it was difficult to marry my passions with my virtue. Little did I realize, I was always on the edge of danger and self-destruction. The more I delved into the Word of God, the more affirmed I was in God's call on my life; but somehow my call and the journey I was on did not seem compatible. I wanted to have fun and enjoy life and at the same time glorify God. What was wrong with that?

I was all for responsibility; but after work, I had to play. I know that Jesus wept and was a man of sorrows, but laughter is the medicine of the soul. It took several hard lessons for me to find the balance. Then God gave me the most precious treasure I could find. I came to understand that the joy of the Lord was my strength.

I took a deep breath and mustered up all of my resources to walk through the huge gates at the Cinderella ball. With all that I had learned from my stops along the way, I knew that all that glittered was not gold. I made sure I was wearing my beautiful slippers, shining forth the Gospel of peace and Book of Truth, and walked on. They had given me strength to work through my horrible experiences, and they gave me fortitude when heartaches overwhelmed me. Now they would deliver me to my Prince Charming.

As soon as my heart could bear it, I began my dance at the Cinderella ball. By now, I knew I would immediately recognize my Prince Charming and that no one would ever fool me again. It restored my soul to sit by the still waters, and the Book of Truth led me to green pastures. I repented of my foolishness as harsh words echoed in my mind. I was clear now on what I needed to do and where I needed to go. Nothing could stop me now.

There was, however, one step in my journey of which I wasn't aware.

CHAPTER 4

Midnight Hour

The bands of the wicked have robbed me: but I have not
forgotten thy law. At midnight I will rise to give thanks unto
thee because of thy righteous judgments. I am a companion of
all them that fear thee, and of them that keep thy precepts.

—Psalm 119:61–63

In *Ever After*, Cinderella dares to dream that maybe her Prince
Charming really would sweep her away and love her in spite of
her poverty and position. At the ball, she becomes completely
vulnerable with him. She selflessly gives her heart to him and
extends her quivering trust with the news of her deception. In a
fit of rage, her Prince Charming makes a public spectacle of her,
rejects her, and leaves her running from his disapproval. She is
abandoned and rejected on every level by her love, her family, and
society. Suddenly, the clock strikes twelve, and in the wake of her
torment, she leaves one of her glass slippers behind.

It was always in me to be totally transparent even to the point of harm. When I admitted who I was to men at the Cinderella ball, I was laughed to scorn and despised. Shrouded in guilt over my divorce and crippled from a broken heart, I heard the clock strike twelve. Here I was with a two-year-old, no job, ill health, and nothing to show for all of the lessons about men I had worked so diligently to learn. I fervently sought the Book of Truth to find my way.

I had entered into a vow too hastily and had to pay the consequences of my actions. My naivety was simple minded and carried me into the mouth of the lion. I ran into the streets of the world for consolation and acceptance, only to find society spewing forth the fire of hell. At the first taste of love's bitter pill, I did not learn the lesson of the ages and kept going toward the snare of the fowler.

Now the midnight hour had come and the wicked had surrounded me. I had no way out. Who I thought was my Prince Charming had caged me, broken my wings, and shattered my glass slipper—my precious Gospel of peace. Years would pass before I would recoup from such annihilation. How I longed for the safety of my cottage and the protection of my pseudo-fortress. Even the worst of my dreary days in my cottage could not compare to the darkness of this dungeon. Day by day, the circumstances of life chipped away at my being while my soul lay dormant in darkness and despair. I turned to the Book of Truth for sustenance, and it began to weave the dark threads in the tapestry of my life.

In 1987, the divorce rate in America was 21 percent. While it was becoming more common ground among churchgoers, the church was ill-equipped to minister to divorcees. In the middle of the Bible Belt, divorce was still unacceptable, and society defaulted to the woman as the culprit. Don't get me wrong, I still believe divorce is not the best God has for us; but God allowed it because he knew the hardness of men's hearts. It was a very gracious act of God for me to have a bill of divorcement in the midst of such abuse. But my hopes and dreams were bound up in full-time ministry, which doesn't take too kindly to divorcees. When the clock struck twelve in my life, those hopes and dreams were as shattered as my glass slipper.

I was thrust into the single life with a two-year old baby. I would never be a preacher's wife. I would never administrate a Christian school. I would never know the love of a man. It was a dark hour and dawn was nowhere in sight. The rains drenched me to the bone, and there was no reprieve.

All I could do was sit in the ashes of my circumstances and wait on God to perform some kind of miracle. It was during this time in my life that I met genuine men and understood probably for the first time how real men (many of whom I have mentioned) show forth the attributes of God. My brother-in-law gave me a job, and my church daycare took my daughter in like she was their own. I eventually went to work with the general counsel of our company, who assisted me in the foolish custody battle my ex-husband had filed. Men in my office devoted a weekend to repair my home and make it livable. As my daughter grew, my vice president allowed her to stay in a conference room after school so she wouldn't become a latch-key kid, and my other supervisor was always giving us special monetary gifts to get us through the tough days. Men in my office and at church assisted in tutoring, major purchases, and a myriad of other tasks too overwhelming for a single mom.

Of course, most precious to me during that midnight hour was my friendship with my best friend from college. It was through our friendship that I came to understand a good man even in his failings. As dear to me as any brother, her husband allowed me to experience pure inclusion and support.

In Psalm 68:6, the Lord gave me a verse to carry me through. He promised to "set the solitary in families: he brings out those which are bound with chains: but the rebellious dwell in a dry land." That is exactly what God did for me when He allowed me to be a part of their family.

My best friend's husband was born in the heart of the south and was a vintage '60s hippie. The very first picture I saw of him was with fire red hair down to his waist, a mustache and beard, and numbers stamped on his chest. I have to say that it would have been quite daunting had I not known him when he entered Bible college to become a preacher.

He rose above heroin addiction, jail terms, and a '60s lifestyle and became one of the godliest men I have ever known. He was wild as a March hare and with a temper that could take anyone down, and we became well acquainted when he married my best friend. Oddly enough, we came to realize that we shared a similar temperament and most certainly the same faith. Based on our regard for his wife, a rich friendship grew. I have to admit, however, that it did not come without difficulty. We faced many challenges and disagreements, which I am sure kept my best friend in agony, wondering if she would ever see us talking to each other again.

In the end, ours proved to be a friendship of mutual respect and admiration. He was the type that willingly forsook hearth and home for others. He was giving to a fault and sought to please God in all that he did. He pioneered a thriving work in Cheyenne, Wyoming, where I witnessed them experience poverty beyond belief. Regardless, he persevered, and even in his destitution lent a helping hand to anyone in need. It was always in him to offer even when he didn't have it to give.

He moved from Wyoming to shepherd a congregation of Houstonians who loved him as he loved them. Of all of the attributes he had, his greatest was devotion. He was a strong man and egregious in his passion for his Lord and his family. In a day when leaders are scarce, he could be counted among those who have maintained the leadership characteristics that achieved results. He was honest and direct in his approach and commanded the respect and following of good men and women.

He was a good husband and adored my best friend with the adulation of a princess. He stood by her in sickness and in health, and they salvaged many young lives by opening their home to them in an hour of need. A praying man, he supported me and my daughter with countless intercessions during our darkest and most trying days.

I have found in my lifetime that of all friends made, men have been some of the best. Great men approach friendships with devotion and perspective. Very few relinquish a friendship of any kind for mere power or prestige. They seem to understand the deepest meaning of friendship and have propensity to rise above the petty circumstances that often destroy friendships between women. Such was my friendship with him.

He was a man of God and cherished God as Friend and Father, and I will always be grateful to have shared life with him. Sadly, at the young age of fifty-six, God chose to take him from this life into the realms of glory.

In my darkest hours, I constantly cried out for reprieve, and God would invariably answer by putting men in my life who would show forth His attributes. As I ran from the Cinderella ball, my glass slipper shattered, and I found myself walking barefoot over the hot coals of life. Moment by moment, God began to transform me from a broken chunk of coal into a beautiful, sparkling diamond more precious than even my glass slippers.

Then, one day, on our walk together, you will never believe what I saw.

CHAPTER 5

Acres of Diamonds

But godliness with contentment is great gain.

—1 Timothy 6:5–6

When Cinderella finally won her Prince Charming, the thought of him riding through her own backyard as she threw apples at him became a joyful memory. She had worked that backyard and tended it with every ounce of strength she could muster. She nurtured her relationships there and ensured no intruder would infringe on her beloved farm. Then one day, the prince himself took her father's horse and came riding through, leaving her in his wake. Providentially, Cinderella and her prince met time and time again on that same farm under different circumstances, all the while volleying their differences and disdain for each other.

Just like Cinderella, it wasn't long before the sod under my feet became cultivated and easier to walk. As I looked forward, I failed to look down to see that God had replaced the tough, rocky turf with acres of diamonds. Through the course of my journey, God led me to a very special story that I will never forget. As I pursued a Prince Charming who was becoming more and more obscure, there were some boys that certainly qualified, but I was too ignorant to recognize it. When I bemoaned not having a Prince Charming, God put in my path several men who compensated. And when life was at its worst, godly men stood in the gap to fill the void. Often in our pursuit of happiness, acres of diamonds are in our own backyards just waiting for us to realize all that God has given.

In 1870, a pastor of Grace Baptist Church in Philadelphia presented a lecture he entitled *Acres of Diamonds*. It became so popular that he gave the lecture six thousand more times all over the world. Millions of people paid to hear that famous lecture, and Conwell used most of the proceeds to establish and maintain Temple University.

The lecture told of a man named Al Hafed who lived in ancient Persia. He was very wealthy and had found contentment in all that God had given him. On one occasion, a traveler stopped to visit Al Hafed and told him about a legend of diamonds.

The traveler proceeded to tell him that God sent flames through the cooling crust of earth's creation and made mountains and valleys. When the earth cooled quickly, it produced granite. Silver came out of that which cooled less quickly. That which cooled even less quickly became gold. After gold, diamonds were made.

"Diamonds," he said, "are congealed drops of sunlight!"

Al Hafed could not stop thinking about those diamonds. He knew they must be worth a great fortune. With all of his wealth, Al Hafed went to bed that night a poor man. His discontent had made him realize what he didn't have instead of all he had. He decided he wanted a mine of diamonds so he sold his farm, left his family, and went in search of them. Al Hafed traveled the world depleting his resources and became truly impoverished. In his discontent, Al Hafed cast himself into the ocean to die, a broken and spent man who took his own life in a strange land.

Amazingly, on Al Hafed's farm, a camel was brought into one of the lush gardens to drink. As that camel put its nose down into the clear water of the garden brook, a flash of light shined from the stream. Reaching in, the new owner pulled out a black stone having an eye of light that reflected all the colors of the rainbow. *It resembled the sun congealed in a stone.*

On his way back home, the old traveler stopped again at the same farm to rest. When he saw the stone, he recognized it as a diamond. He told the farmer about the diamonds, and they rushed back to the brook where the first diamond was found. There, they stirred up the white sands with their fingers and found more diamonds than they could have ever imagined. The discovery was the famed diamond mines of Golconda, some of the richest diamond mines of all time.

Had Al Hafed remained at home and dug in his own garden, instead of wretchedness, starvation, poverty, and death in a strange land, he would have had "acres of diamonds," but his discontent pulled him away from the very best that God had for him. Every shovelful they dug up on that old farm brought up wonderful diamonds, some of which have decorated the crowns of many of the world's monarchs.

After the Cinderella ball, I ran back to my cottage. I was so hurt and dismayed, I didn't even recognize the moat and the fire-breathing dragon. They were trivial compared to what I had experienced. Without even realizing it, I was searching for diamonds that could never be found from discontentment. I was looking for a Prince Charming that was only in fairy tales. My definition of love and romance was skewed with a dream about someone who didn't exist.

I traveled the world and entered its taverns looking for love. I was so discontent with all God had put in my path, I kept looking beyond my own acres of diamonds. By the time I had reached my cottage, all that really mattered was there. It was in my utopia that I found contentment in God's will for my life. Sparkling streams of diamonds adorned my attitude, and God gave me a new countenance. His face shined upon me with favor, and He showed me a love I had ignored and taken for granted. The sweet fruits of God's Spirit filled me with a new-found appreciation for all I had experienced.

It was in my own backyard that I discovered how much God had protected me from my own way. He anchored my soul when I fought Him and patiently waited when I pushed Him away. When I thought He wasn't sufficient for my needs and wants, I foolishly thought I could find it elsewhere; yet He loved me still. He refused to allow me to fall off the precipice of Satan's cruel scheme and put a hedge of protection around me that kept me on His path.

One glorious day when the sun shined so bright on my tattered heart, I realized God had led me back to my own acres of diamonds, which appeared now to be the most beautiful castle in the world. It had taken on a whole new look, and I saw a beauty I had never seen before. I ran through the fields and found a sparkling diamond that the Lord pointed out just for me. The moat had been cleaned out and glimmered with the glorious luster of glass. Society was nowhere to be found, and no traces remained of him having ever been there. What I used to think was a cold, dark room was now a safe haven of sunshine and tranquility.

My fairy tale began and ended in the place where God put His name, and the possibility exists that I will live.

CHAPTER 6

Happily Ever After

Behold, we count them happy which endure. Ye have
heard of the patience of Job, and have seen the end of the
Lord; that the Lord is very pitiful, and of tender mercy.

—James 5:11

As Cinderella and her prince embrace, they tease each other about
the likeness of her portrait that Leonardo da Vinci had painted
of her. Her prince laughingly tells her that they are supposed
to live happily ever after. With remarkable repose, she replies,
"Says who?"

It's true. There is no written rule that says we are supposed to live
happily ever after. In fact, that is truly the myth behind the legend
of Cinderella. Life offers no guarantee of happily ever after on this
earth. Even Christ told His disciples to expect persecution, torture,
ostracism, and yes, even death in this life. Happily ever after is a

temporary moment that is fleeting. It is built on happiness, which is a temporal emotion that blows with the winds of time.

Discovering that truth became a surreal reality as I entered midlife. Jesus Christ lovingly reached down and delivered me from my own self-destruction and the evil hands that sought to destroy me. Through my association with earthly men, Christ Himself became the epitome of all my dreams and has far exceeded my imaginations as He became my Prince Charming. All of those great attributes in the men God had put in my life were fulfilled in Christ Himself.

It may sound trite that I have accepted Christ as my Prince Charming since He sits on the right-hand throne of God; but since He is perfect in every way, He could not possibly fail me. What about those women who are in relationships with men—women who are trying to deal with their own broken relationships and trying to keep them together?

That's the beauty of making Christ your Prince Charming. Since He (and only He) can meet all of the criteria, He enhances every human relationship we are in. He blankets our attitudes with contentment and humility as we recognize our own frailties and what we bring to the table in all of our relationships.

This one Man's life has furnished the theme for more songs, books, poems, and paintings than any other person or event in history. Thousands of colleges, hospitals, orphanages, and other institutions have been founded in honor of this one who gave His life for us. All the armies that ever marched, all the navies that ever sailed, all the governments that ever sat, all the kings that ever reigned have not changed the course of history as much as this one solitary man.

It was in that midnight hour that I recognized the one Man that has been dearer to me than any man in my life. His name is Jesus Christ. At the age of four years old, He tugged at my heart's door and beckoned me to come to Him. With the faith of a child, I trustingly jumped into His arms, never to be dropped again.

Lest there be any misunderstanding, even though Jesus Christ lived as a man, walked in the person of a man and died the death of a man, He is more than just a Man. He is Savior and is alive today. Regardless of your belief system or your faith, may I introduce you to one who is faithful, kind, loving, and good. He will never leave or forsake, and He provides complete fulfillment to any woman or man who has been abandoned or brokenhearted.

He promises to defend the borders of the widow, to protect the widow and the orphan, and to set the solitary in families. He is a Father to the fatherless and a Husband to that woman who has been deserted. He has more than met these wonderful promises for my daughter and me. I have been a single parent most of my adult life, and without exception, Jesus Christ has taken care of us both.

Many of the ways in which He has protected me has been through the men mentioned in this book. When a woman loses her dream or is disappointed, Jesus Christ is sufficient. It is difficult to understand how, knowing that He is not a Man as we understand in human terms, but He *is* alive and He lives in the hearts of those who will accept His unconditional love and endless mercy.

So often in my loneliest of times, I would look to the Lover of my soul for solace and comfort. He would hold my weary head with His left hand and embrace me with His right arm. On days that I would feel like a fifth wheel and a couples' society would not open its arms to me, Jesus Christ set me in families that loved me as their own and gave me a place higher than that of a family member. When I was at my wit's end with raising a pubescent daughter and had no man to turn to, Jesus Christ would provide someone to reach her and penetrate her thinking.

Many say He is dead and can no longer impact the lives of those in the twenty-first century. They are wrong. He lives in the hearts and lives of every Christian believer and can fill the emptiness of any woman hurt by thoughtless men or any man hurt by thoughtless women. He gives more grace as the burden grows greater. To multiplied trials, He gives multiplied mercy. His love knows no measure, and His peace passes all understanding. He gives and gives and gives again.

Of all the men I've ever known, Jesus Christ stands supreme. If ever you met a man, meet Him today. Simply recognize that you are a sinner and *need* a Savior (Romans 3:23). Realize that the gift of eternal life awaits you for the asking (Romans 6:23). Accept that gift only in and through Jesus Christ by confessing the need for a Savior because of sin. By believing in your heart that Jesus Christ has conquered sin and was raised from the grave to take away the sting of death, you, too, can know Him as Savior. He has come to seek and to save those who are lost (Romans 10:9–10). This is a Man you will never regret meeting.

Together, we walk side-by-side in every circumstance of life, and I am given extraordinary gifts of love and redemption. We talk together in the cool of the garden as He imparts to me the riches of a life more abundant. He restores my soul with His very breath of life. His embrace rivals none other, and His patience and kindness exceed any I have ever known. He gently helps me rise above my weaknesses and is so very patient with my inadequacies. He has taken my soul to such raptures that I can hardly remember the midnight hour of my despair.

In my daily walks with Him, I slowly regained my strength. My legs now carry me almost as far as before. Except for the scars, it is hardly noticeable that I had been crippled and paralyzed. For the first time in a long time, my heart thrilled with excitement as the resurgence of life penetrated my entire being. God had taken me full circle in my search for my Prince Charming, and He was there all along in my own backyard.

I knelt in adoration of one who loved me in my unloveliness. He stayed by my side even when I longed after another. He redeemed me from the clutches of abuse and unfathomable pain. He refused to let me go even when I fought to be released. He promised to love me in sickness and in health, in poverty and in wealth; even death cannot part us.

Entering into a relationship with Christ as our Prince Charming brings more than anyone can know. We hear psychologists tell us that interacting with others in a *healthy* way makes for a great union. Too many times, we bring untold baggage into our relationships with men, thereby creating *unhealthy* relationships. We hope against hope that they will relieve us of the burdens we bear. If they don't, we throw it on them and crush our hopes of a strong union.

If Jesus Christ is our priority and first love, He carries our baggage for us. His yoke is light. A human relationship can only be enhanced when we let Him carry the weight of our lives' woes. Whether it is a friendship, marriage, or family relationships, when Christ is first, joy abounds. Finding contentment with godliness is great gain in all of our relationships when Jesus Christ is on the throne of our hearts.

The single life is not utopia. There are still men who treat me with no respect and take advantage of my naivety. My happily ever after will probably not occur until heaven. But there is praise that rises above the ashes and resounds in glorious acclaim. Weeping may endure for a moment, but joy comes in the morning. Even in the midst of their shattered, lonely lives, the apostles gave their all to further the cause of Christ on this earth. The gleam in their eyes as they faced death was the glory of heaven.

I have found my Prince Charming in a way I never dreamed. I never believed my journey would lead me to such fulfillment in life. God has replaced my shattered glass slipper with beautiful acres of diamonds in my life and in my heart. He walked through the fire protecting me from the flames with hands of mercy. My indiscretions and simplemindedness induced His pity for me, and He allowed me to see the error of my ways without letting me fall into destruction.

As I began to drown in the torrential flood waters of life, He lovingly dropped down His lifeline to me and then hid me in the cleft of His Rock for safety. The power and love of Jesus Christ nursed me back to health when all I wanted to do was die, and His enduring patience brought me through the valley of the shadow of death. Day by day my Prince Charming proves Himself to me in new and different ways, especially in my relationships.

> He is the great Creator of Genesis breathing His own breath of life into the soul of man. He is the Deliverer of Exodus redeeming His people from tyranny and bondage. He is the Law-giver of Leviticus revealing to mankind the need for a Savior. He is the Record Keeper of Numbers extending His grace over and over again. He is the Historian of Deuteronomy reviewing the countless evidences of His tender mercies. He is the Mighty Victor of Joshua delivering the enemy into the hands of His people by His own power. He is Judge of Judges ruling with majesty and justice. He is the Blessed Kinsman-Redeemer of Ruth loving to the uttermost them that are lost. He is the Prophet of Samuel revealing Himself to foolish man. He is the King of Kings surveying His kingdom to find

but one righteous among us. He is the Author of Chronicles as He sets His time table in motion for every knee to bow and every tongue to confess that He is Lord. He is the Master Builder of Ezra raising up His Church which the gates of Hell will not prevail against. He is the Fortress of Nehemiah surrounding His people with the mighty fortress of His presence. He is the Mighty Sovereign of Esther making all things work together for good to them who love the Lord. He is the Patience of Job waiting for the complete redemption of those He loves. He is the Song of the Psalms heralding the depths of His love to all generations. He is the Wisdom of Proverbs dividing asunder the thoughts and intents of the heart of mankind. He is the Lover of Solomon's Song intimately pursuing those He loves. He is Holy, Holy, Holy in Isaiah sounding out His warnings of judgment and chastisement upon a rebellious and stiff-necked people. He is the Weeping Prophet of Jeremiah grieving over the rejection of His own. He is the Teardrops of Lamentations preserving every tear in His vials as a reminder. He is the Wheel of Ezekiel turning the tide of judgment upon evil. He is the Lion of Judah in Daniel shutting the mouths of those creatures of destruction. He is the Loving Husband of Hosea forgiving our infidelities. He is the Sounding Call of Zion in Joel offering one final act of mercy upon a people who have chosen gods made from the hands of man. He is the Treader of the grapes of wrath in Amos crushing the hearts of man that He might salvage some. He is the Ambassador of Obadiah offering a last warning to a godless state. He is the Call of Jonah upon a life tempered with prejudice and hate. He is the Witness of Micah emerging forth from His holy temple to reach His godless people. He is the Vindicator of Nahum extracting vengeance on evildoers. He is the Tender Mercy of Habakkuk heeding the cries for revival among His people. He is the Consuming Fire of Zephaniah reaching unto the far corners of the Earth to make His way known. He is the Signet of Haggai marking His own for the harvest. He is the Suitor of Zechariah calling His own back into His embrace. He is the Final Voice of Malachi before the 400 years of silence introduces the Christ Child. He is the New Testament completely fulfilling every prophecy, every meaning, and every law given unto man. He is the Great I AM; and He loves even me![4]

He may choose to send me a life partner on earth, and He may not. I have learned to accept His choices for me, which have brought me total peace. His Person drives my heart to want more of Him every day in every way. I lift mine eyes unto the hills from whence cometh my help until someday.

---

[4] Charles Spurgeon Notes. http://spurgeongems.org/sermons.htm

CHAPTER 7

Somewhere Over the Rainbow

Let not your heart be troubled: ye believe in God, believe also in me. In my Father's house are many mansions: if it were not so, I would have told you. I go to prepare a place for you. And if I go and prepare a place for you, I will come again, and receive you unto myself; that where I am, there ye may be also.

—John 14:1–3

After Cinderella marries her Prince Charming and wears his crown, she has opportunity to bring retribution on her wicked stepmother. While she could have ordered her death, instead Cinderella orders that her stepmother be treated as she was treated. To preface her indictment, Cinderella tells her stepmother that after that, she will never think of her again.

Since discovering the Lover of my soul, life has taken on a completely new perspective from before. I can look at others who have hurt me and forgive them because He first forgave me! I can never hate those who have caused my suffering because I caused His suffering! I can truly entrust the outcome of wickedness to the Righteous One who is sovereign.

There is coming a day when I will never think of this life again except for what I did for Christ. I have seen the blessed hope that I had taken so for granted in the beginning. I have opened my heart to the dream of hereafter. If this life was all there was, I would have fallen into hopelessness; but when I set my affection on things that are above, my perspective is eternal, and my dreams are no longer a fairy tale. His promises make my dreams real with the reality that they will someday come true.

Every time I see a rainbow, I am comforted by His promise of protection. Every time I feel the breeze on my face, I am reminded of the power of the Holy Spirit that lives within me. Every time I see the wheat fields white unto harvest, I long for others to know the peace and joy He has given me. With each passing moment, God puts reminders in my path that life is but a vapor and eternity waits somewhere over the rainbow.

The Lover of my soul has stamped His identity in my heart and given me the haven of His church. He has used me in ways beyond my comprehension to bring others to the saving knowledge of His redeeming love. His amazing grace has filled my heart with praise, and life's trials are but for a moment.

Those dreams that I thought were lost to me have been multiplied. God has more than blessed me with ministry opportunities since I have taken Him as my Prince Charming. He has allowed me to travel the world ministering to women everywhere. He has given beauty for ashes, the oil of joy for mourning, and the garment of praise for the spirit of heaviness. He has restored unto me all that I have lost and more with four adorable grandchildren and a son-in-law who is dearer to me than a son.

I am grieved when I consider the testimony of discontent I have left with those on my journey back. Days and even years of hurt and betrayal produced anger and disdain in my heart. Many of my days were laced with cynicism and disregard for what others were going through. There were even times when I stifled relationships God intended me to embrace as a testimony to Him. In finding my Prince Charming, I myself have caused similar hurts and betrayals that were imposed upon me.

God has not let me forget how I was on my journey. He reminds me almost daily of the repercussions of failing to place Him on the throne of my life. It is my prayer that those I have hurt or slighted may find through their circumstances the beauty of His holiness. I pray they can look past the darkness of the way they were treated and find solace in the one who bore all those pains for us.

Dear reader, you too can know the Prince Charming of the ages who will never leave you or forsake you. Jesus Christ will meet every expectation you could possibly have and become the core of your healthy relationships. He gently knocks on the door of every heart, asking to come in to fellowship with those He loves. To know Him is to love Him. Once He is placed on the throne of a heart, He becomes all things necessary and is sufficient. Through Him, earthly relationships glorify Him.

A Hollywood dream is just that when we go our own way in relationships or impose our own desires. Romance is diminished when what drives our romance is human and not eternal. Magic reaps no reward when we allow His infinite blessings to be squandered on the temporary. The pot of gold at the end of the rainbow will dissipate if we spend our wealth in our relationships on self and not for God's honor and glory.

Do I still look at life through rose-colored glasses? Could it be that I have lost sight of reality in the midst of my dark despair? Yes, I do still look through rose-colored glasses; but they are not the same glasses I wore at the beginning of my journey. I have seen my Rose of Sharon wear a crown of thorns for me. I have seen the pain He suffered for me and the unconditional love He has for me. Now I see through a glass darkly, but soon it will be face-to-face. Now I know in part, but soon I will know as I am known.

My Prince Charming has gone to prepare a place for me in heaven. He has called it a mansion—my very own castle. But nothing will compare to living with Him through eternity. He will never leave me or forsake me. He will be the Light of Heaven, and there will be no more pain, no more tears, no more night. He will wipe away all tears from my eyes, and the brutal things I experienced here on earth will be counted for righteousness to Him who is righteous.

My glass slipper has broken and has been replaced with the sparkling diamonds of love, joy, peace, longsuffering, gentleness, goodness, faith, temperance, and meekness. When your glass slipper breaks, dear reader, let God transform your purpose for living. Let God give you acres of diamonds and streams of gold. Only He can make life worth living, and by making Jesus Christ your Prince Charming, new meaning will fill your soul. Make Him the Prince Charming you always dreamed about.

When your glass slipper breaks, He is standing ready to heal.

> *He that dwelleth in the secret place of the most High*
> *shall abide under the shadow of the Almighty.*
> *I will say of the LORD, He is my refuge and my*
> *fortress: my God; in him will I trust.*
> *Surely he shall deliver thee from the snare of the*
> *fowler, and from the noisome pestilence.*
> *He shall cover thee with his feathers, and under his wings*
> *shalt thou trust: his truth shall be thy shield and buckler.*

— Psalm 91:1-4

Printed in the United States
By Bookmasters